Color Companion for the Digital Artist

AGAINST THE CLOCK
mastering graphic technology

PEARSON
Prentice Hall

Upper Saddle River, NJ 07458

VP/Publisher: Natalie E. Anderson
Associate Director, IT Product Development: Melonie Salvati
Executive Editor: Steven Elliot
Assistant Editor: Allison Marcus
Marketing Manager: Steven Rutberg
Marketing Assistant: Barrie Reinhold
Associate Director of Production and Manufacturing: Vincent Scelta
Manager, Production: Gail Steier de Acevedo
Production Project Manager: Natacha St. Hill Moore
Manufacturing Buyer: Natacha St. Hill Moore
Composition: Against The Clock, Inc.
Design Director: Maria Lange
Design Coordinator: Christopher Kossa
Cover Design: LaFortezza Design Group, Inc.
Printer/Binder: Quebecor World-Taunton
Cover Printer: Phoenix Color Corp.

Pearson Education LTD.
Pearson Education Australia PTY, Limited
Pearson Education Singapore, Pte. Ltd
Pearson Education North Asia Ltd
Pearson Education Canada, Ltd.
Pearson Educación de Mexico, S.A. de C.V.
Pearson Education — Japan
Pearson Education Malaysia, Pte. Ltd
Pearson Education, Upper Saddle River, New Jersey

PEARSON
Prentice Hall

10 9 8 7 6 5 4 3 2 1

ISBN 0-13-097524-9

Contents

Preface

The *Against The Clock Companion Series* offers insight into fundamental artistic issues. It covers the details of broad design topics such as:

- The basic rules of good design,
- The proper and effective use of color,
- The history and application of typography,
- The principles underlying proven and compelling Web site design.

The *Against The Clock Companion Series* works together with application-specific libraries of training and skills-development books. The books in the series provide background in fundamental design and artistic issues. They complement the hands-on, skills-based approach of the Against The Clock and other applications titles. The series:

- Contains **richly illustrated real-world examples** of commercial and institutional artwork, designs, packaging, and other creative assignments;
- Provides the reasoning behind the **creative strategies, production methodologies, and distribution models** — in the words of the artists who provided them;
- Addresses the four most important disciplines critical to successful use of computer arts applications: **design, color, typography, and Web page design**;
- Presents the material in a **friendly and easy-to-understand manner**, rather than relying on technical jargon or obsolete terminology.

The books in the Companion Series are:

- *Design Companion for the Digital Artist* (ISBN: 0-13-091237-9)
- *Typography Companion for the Digital Artist* (ISBN: 0-13-040993-6)
- *Web Design Companion for the Digital Artist* (ISBN: 0-13-097355-6)
- *Color Companion for the Digital Artist* (ISBN: 0-13-097524-9)
- *Writing Companion for the Digital Artist* (ISBN: 0-13-112485-4)

We hope that you'll find the books as effective and useful as we found them exciting and fun to develop. As always, we welcome any comments you might have that will make the next editions of the books even better. Please feel free to contact us at courseware@againsttheclock.com.

About Against The Clock

Against The Clock (ATC) was founded in 1990 and went on to become one of the nation's leading systems integration and training firms. The organization, founded by Ellenn Behoriam, specialized in developing custom training materials for clients such as L.L. Bean, *The New England Journal of Medicine*, the Smithsonian, the National Education Association, *Air & Space Magazine*, Publishers Clearing House, the National Wildlife Society, Home Shopping Network, and many others.

Building on their lengthy experience creating focused and structured training materials, ATC's management team began working with major publishers in the mid-nineties to produce high-quality application and workflow-specific training aids. In 1996, ATC introduced the highly popular "Creative Techniques" series, which focused on real-world examples of award-winning commercial design, imaging, and Web page development. Working with Adobe Press, they also developed successful management books, including *Workflow Reengineering*, which won the IDIA award as most effective book of the year in 1997.

In 1998, the company entered into a long-term relationship with Prentice Hall/Pearson Education. This relationship allows ATC to focus on bringing high-quality content to the marketplace to address up-to-the-minute software releases. The Against The Clock library has grown to include over 35 titles — focusing on all aspects of computer arts. From illustration to Web site design, from image to animation, and from page layout to effective production techniques, the series is highly-regarded and is recognized as one of the most powerful teaching and training tools in the industry.

Against The Clock, Inc. is located in Tampa, Florida and can be found on the Web at www.againsttheclock.com.

Acknowledgements

I would like to thank the writers, editors, illustrators and production staff who have worked long and hard to complete the Against The Clock series.

Thank you to our technical team of teaching professionals whose comments and expertise contributed to the success of this book, including Doris Anton of Wichita Area Technical College; Dee Colvin of University of North Florida; Rainer Fleschner of Moraine Park Technical College; and Carin Murphy of Des Moines Area Community College.

Finally, a big thanks to David Broudy of Jostens, Inc. who provided much of the information for the color management and proofing chapters.

About the Author

Erika Kendra earned a BA in History and a BA in English Literature from the University of Pittsburgh. She began her career in the graphic communication industry as an editor at Graphic Arts Technical Foundation. She moved to Los Angeles in 2000 and now works as an a freelance editor, writer, and designer. She also provides desktop-publishing training and prepress consulting for the printing industry. When she isn't working, she can usually be found prowling in book stores or enjoying the southern California sun.

Erika is the author of several Against The Clock titles, including *QuarkXPress: Introduction to Electronic Documents*; *QuarkXPress: Advanced Electronic Documents*; *Preflight and File Preparation*; and *Adobe PageMaker: Creating Electronic Documents*. She is also the co-author of *Adobe Photoshop: Advanced Digital Imaging* and the *Design Companion for the Digital Artist.*

Introduction

Color is a basic concept that we begin experimenting with in early childhood. To complete our earliest art projects — crayons at the ready — we learned that mixing the yellow crayon with the blue one makes green, yellow and red make orange, and red and blue make purple. If you mix all three, you get an ugly dark brown that usually ends up in the trash. Designing with color, however, is more complex than what you learned in preschool.

As a graphic designer, your job is to visually communicate an idea, whether in print, on television, on the Internet, or with some other medium. Effective use of color is part artistry, part psychology, part theory, part science, and part mechanics. It is not enough to drop a big red dot on the page and call it a day. You have to know why red is the best choice; how people will react to red; how the red will interact with other colors and in different places; and how to recreate the red in the medium for which you are designing.

When we developed the initial outline for this book, someone asked, "Are you going to have a chapter about digital color?" Our immediate response was, "Of course." Throughout the development process, however, it became clear that the idea of "digital color" is too broad to isolate in a single chapter; graphic design is largely a digital process. As a result, the entire book discusses digital color — the science and theory behind it, the tools we use to create it, the media used to output it, and the issues related to printing it.

It is important to note that each chapter in this book — and in many cases, each *section* of each chapter — could be expanded to hundreds of pages. Because it would be impossible to explain every detail in a single book, we focus on the issues you need to understand to effectively design with color. Our goal is to present an accessible, understandable, and practical explanation of color reproduction.

CHAPTER 1

A Brief History of Visual Communication

Some of the earliest existing examples of written communication have been preserved in the pictographic writings (or *hieroglyphics*) of ancient Egypt. Messages were carved into stone tablets, written on papyrus scrolls, and in many cases carved on tomb walls. The media used for communicating evolved over time — the earliest rock carvings and paintings gave way to writing on animal skins, clay tablets, vellum, fine papyrus; eventually these evolved into the high-quality papers (and low-quality newsprint) that we use today.

The lavish use of color — especially in some of the funerary writings on papyrus — is believed to be an indication of the power and popularity of the person who was buried in a specific tomb.

For thousands of years, documents were painstakingly written and copied by hand, character by character. In those days, the rule for writing was straightforward — the words simply had to be captured accurately. Many people who could "write" could not, in fact, read the words; they merely reproduced the shapes of the letters on a page.

Illumination

For a largely illiterate culture, communication relied heavily on word of mouth. Alternatively, information — histories, legal codes, and religious ideas — could be spread through the use of images. Stories were told through pictures — woven into tapestries, painted on walls, drawn on vellum. These forms of storytelling predate any realistic means of mass production, yet color figures prominently in most surviving examples. Of course it's impossible to make a 700-page painting, so events had to be condensed into symbolic images. In fact, color was not only added for aesthetic effect, but assisted the storyteller in communicating more complex ideas through symbolism. A person wearing blue, for example, symbolized a member of a religious group; anyone wearing red was of noble birth; those wearing purple were most likely royalty.

Medieval documents give us many very sophisticated examples of this type of visual communication. *Illuminations*, or the beautiful colored illustrations we find in documents that survive from the medieval period, were added by artistically talented monks to embellish the hand-written pages.

Many documents were embellished by hand illumination, which represented important stories in a visual and often colorful depiction.

Because every copy of a document was hand-written, the cost of owning printed material was prohibitive for all but the extremely wealthy. In those early societies, written language was often limited to the priests and scribes, who became the writers and readers of the written word. Most of the aristocracy was, in fact, illiterate, relying instead upon the clerics to record and communicate information. While we applaud the skills of these early publishers, we also note that these people had great power as the sole writers and readers of the recorded word. They acted as spokespeople and interpreters for the gods and rulers of that society, thereby controlling public belief, policy, and opinion.

Automating the Publishing Process

A revolution occurred in the mid-1400s that would eventually make wide-scale publishing a reality. In 1450, Johannes Gutenberg changed forever the way people communicate when he invented a printing press that used movable metal type, making it easier to make multiple copies of documents. The process involved manually coating metal castings of type with ink, and then pressing those plates against the paper with a lever or screw, creating an imprint of the plate on the paper. Modern printing was born. Documents would become public because they could be produced in sufficient quantity to be distributed to large groups of people, and could be afforded by those other than the very wealthy.

> Historical records suggest that the Koreans were printing with moveable type fifty years prior to Gutenberg, but he is still credited with the invention.

Gutenberg's invention, despite its impact on the way we communicate, effectively removed color from most documents. Some early printed documents were still illuminated by hand, but the time-consuming process defeated the purpose of being able to quickly reproduce multiple copies; illumination eventually devolved into a lost art. Images, when they were included in printed documents, were engraved into metal blocks and printed in black ink.

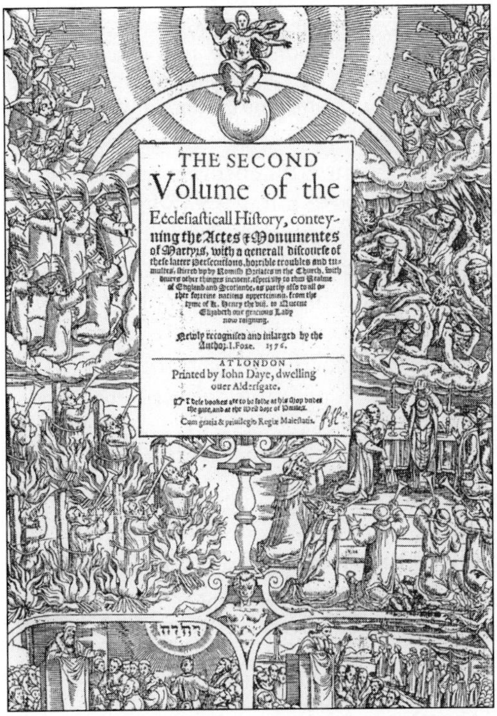
THE SECOND
Volume of the
Ecclesiasticall History, conteyning the Actes & Monumentes of Martyrs, with a generall discourse of these latter Persecutions, horrible troubles and tumultes, stirred up by Romish Prelates in the Church, with divers other thinges incident, especially to this Realme of England and Scotlande, as partly also to all other foreine nations appertaining, from the tyme of K. Henry the viii. to Queene Elizabeth our gracious Lady now raigning.
Newly recognised and inlarged by the Author. I. Foxe. 1576.
AT LONDON
Printed by Iohn Daye, dwelling over Aldersgate.
These bookes are to be solde at his shop under the gate, and at the West dore of Paules.
Cum gratia & privilegio Regiæ Maiestatis.

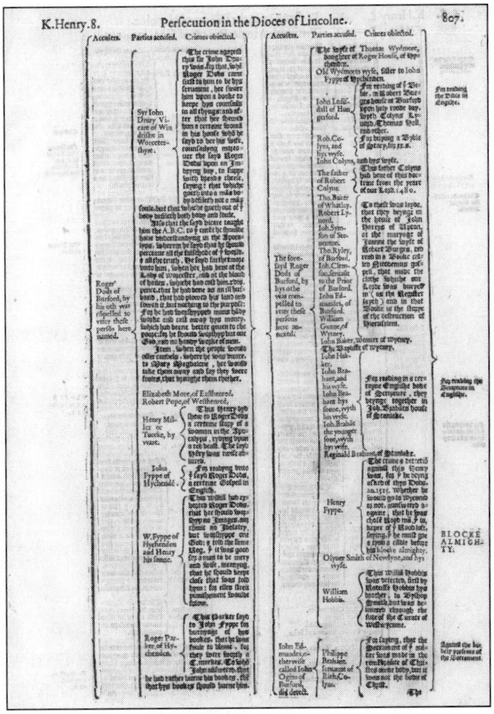
K.Henry.8. Persecution in the Dioces of Lincolne. 807.
Accusers. Parties accused. Crimes obiected.

The often-intricate engravings that were added to printed documents were reproduced only in black. The right image shows the more common appearance of a printed page, which included only text and the occasional line.

Printing allowed easier and (comparatively) more affordable access to written documents, which in turn allowed literacy to flourish; the allegorical embroidery and paintings that were once the only way to relay information to an illiterate populace eventually became forms of art rather than communication.

As printing evolved, documents were typically illustrated with engravings that we think of as line art. Color was often added by hand using watercolor paints after the document was printed.

Although the basic concept of printing — ink applied to a raised surface, then literally *pressed* onto paper — would not change over the next few centuries, a number of improvements were made to the original approach. In 1710, Jakob LeBlon developed a three-color printing process that finally allowed the mechanical reproduction of color. Later in the same century, Alois Senefelder would experiment with different methods of printing, eventually inventing lithography around 1798.

Throughout the nineteenth and early twentieth centuries, printing rapidly evolved into the processes we still use today. In 1855, Alphonse-Louis Poitevin invented photolithography using the principles that were simultaneously evolving into photography as we know it. The *halftone process*, which is still used to print photographs, was developed at the same time so photographs could be easily reproduced as part of the printing process. In 1893, process-color printing was successfully introduced, leading the way to printing color photographs in the early twentieth century.

Photography

The birth of modern photography is historically credited to Louis Daguerre. The *daguerreotype* method, introduced in 1839, worked by exposing a silver plate to iodine vapors. The chemical reaction resulted in a light-sensitive layer of silver iodide on the plate, which was exposed to light in a camera. After exposure, the silver plate was exposed to mercury vapor and the unexposed silver iodide was removed from the plate with a salt solution to create the image.

At the same time Daguerre was exposing silver plates, William Henry Fox Talbot invented the *calotype* (from the Greek "kalos," meaning beautiful). This process used paper treated with silver iodide, which was exposed with a camera and developed in gallic acid. A negative image was captured on the treated paper, which was then transferred to a second special paper to create the positive image. Talbot's photographs did not have the same quality as those produced with the daguerreotype method, largely due to the quality and graininess of the paper used for capturing negatives. The concept of the calotype, however, would eventually lead to photography as we know it, where multiple prints are made from a single negative film image.

Daguerreotypes (above) and tintypes (right) were two early forms of photography.

These photos were not retouched, to show how the early photographs can darken over time.

Early photographs were often hand painted to add color.

Throughout the nineteenth century, numerous improvements were made to these early versions of photography. In 1848, Claude Felix Abel Niepce de Saint-Victor discovered that albumen, a protein found in egg whites, allowed light-sensitive chemicals to develop on a glass plate instead of the paper used in Talbot's original invention. In 1851, Frederick Scott Archer replaced the albumen used on glass plates with collodion (cellulose nitrate, the same explosive substance that later made moving pictures so dangerous). The plates had to be exposed and developed while the plate coating was still wet, hence the process was called "wet-plate photography."

The wet-plate process was very popular with some professional photographers, but was limited because of the need to develop exposed plates while they were wet. In 1871, Richard Maddox replaced the collodion with a gelatin substance that did not require the immediate exposure of the wet-plate process. John Corbutt invented a cellulose photographic film in 1887 to replace plates. George Eastman introduced roll film and the first Kodak camera in 1888; the film was sent — still in the camera — to be developed.

COLOR PHOTOGRAPHY

Physicist James Clerk Maxwell began experimenting with color photography in 1855. The first color photograph was produced by photographing the same image three times through a series of red, green, and blue filters. The three distinct images were turned into slides and projected through three different projectors using the appropriate color filters. When the three projected images were focused and registered to one another, the result was a full-color image.

In 1869, Arthur-Louis Ducos du Hauron described the subtractive color method, which changed the direction of color photography. Ducos du Hauron suggested film could be coated with three layers of emulsion that were each sensitive to a different primary color. After the negatives were processed, the technique would produce a full-color positive transparency. Ducos du Hauron's theories, however, would not be practically applied for many years because the emulsions used during his lifetime were not sensitive enough to the green and red areas of the spectrum. Panchromatic film, sensitive enough to capture all areas of the color spectrum, was developed around the turn of the century.

Ducos du Hauron's contributions to color photography also included the Helio Chromatic camera, which captured three separate negatives inside a camera with a single exposure. This type of photograph was able to reproduce the full range of colors, but still required the combination of three separate images to create the single color composite.

In 1873 John Joly developed a system that was able to capture color in a single image, using a screen of microscopic red, green, and blue stripes placed in front of a black-and-white plate. Using this process, a single negative could be developed into a positive image and projected in color.

Louis and Auguste Lumière introduced the Autochrome process in 1904, which replaced Joly's striped screen with color dots made of red, green, and blue potato starch particles. In 1907, the Lumière brothers introduced the Autochrome photographic plate, which is considered to be the first commercially successful color photographic plate. In 1914, Agfa replaced the starch particles used in the Autochrome plates with colored resin particles. Agfa began marketing the new plates in 1916 and further refined the process in 1923.

The most significant change in color photography began in 1912 when experiments generated dyes within the film emulsion during the development process instead of after the film or plates were developed. The main difficulty with this *dye-coupling* technique was the tendency of the dyes to bleed into the other emulsion layers, which caused color shifts and bad results.

An early Autochrome photograph.

If you look closely, you can see the starch particles.

After experimenting with different methods for three-emulsion film, Leopold Mannes and Leopold Godowsky (working for Kodak Research Laboratories) abandoned the idea of isolating dyes to specific emulsion layers, and researched the possibility of using coloring agents in developing solutions. Kodak introduced the first modern, three-emulsion color film, Kodachrome, in 1935. The Kodachrome development process was so complicated, however, that only a few labs were able to support the film.

Gustav Wilmanns and Wilhelm Schneider, who had begun the experiments with dye-coupling film for Agfa, finally overcame the dye-migration problem, enabling Agfa to introduce Agfacolor Neu in 1936. This became the foundation for all modern film-based photographic processes. (Kodak introduced the competitive Ektacolor film in 1941.)

Color in Motion

As photography evolved into a commercially viable method for capturing still images, pioneers in the industry worked to expand the concept to capture motion. The invention of flexible cellulose film for photography also allowed experimentation to begin with film-based motion-picture photography.

Motion pictures became a commercial reality in 1891, when William Dickson ran strips of George Eastman's 35-mm cellulose film through Thomas Edison's Kinetograph camera. In 1896, the first movies in the United States — one-minute shorts — were projected through a Vitascope projector.

The earliest film-based motion pictures were dangerous exhibitions. The cellulose nitrate film was projected through hydrogen-oxygen burning lamps, hand-cranked at 16 frames per second, creating a potentially explosive combination. Safety film (cellulose acetate) was developed in 1908 and a motor was added to the projector in 1915, allowing longer motion pictures to be developed.

By the 1920s, motion pictures had become the primary form of entertainment in the world. The film industry soon began to experiment with color, producing spectacular results that changed the future of the entertainment industry.

IN LIVING COLOR

A variety of color processes had been used for motion pictures since 1896. In 1915, Herbert Kalmus established Technicolor Corporation, which fused together projections from a red filter and a blue-green filter to create full color on the screen. *The Gulf Between*, shown in 1917, was the first film to use the additive color process; it was not terribly successful because the projectionist had to be able to carefully register the two projections on the screen.

The Technicolor process would change at least three times in fifteen years, until the three-color imbibation process was developed in 1932. A special camera simultaneously captured images on red, green, and blue film rolls, which were later fused together into a single print. This method was adopted by Disney, which used the Technicolor process for the animated *Flowers and Trees* in 1932. The first non-animated three-color film, *La Cucaracha* (a short), appeared in 1934. The following year, *Becky Sharp* became the first feature-length non-animated color motion picture.

Despite the pioneering developments, the Technicolor process was largely relegated to animated projects such as *Snow White and the Seven Dwarfs* (1937) and big-budget productions like *Gone with the Wind* (1939) because the cumbersome Technicolor camera weighed more than 500 pounds and required a substantial amount of light to get proper exposure.

Kodak's Eastmancolor print process — which placed layers of colored dyes on a single strip of film — ended Technicolor's monopoly on the color market in the early 1950s. By 1955, half of the films released used Eastmancolor, which would also be the basis for processes such as Warnercolor, Color by De Luxe, and Metrocolor.

A frame from ***The Blooming Desert****, using the three-color Technicolor process.*

Conclusion

Color has been an integral part of visual communication for millennia. Long before we even conceived of televisions or digital cameras, color was used to convey ideas such as rank, religion, and identity. In comparison, color reproduction has a relatively short history, but one that continues to change with the introduction of new technology. Color communication, whether in print or on screen, is a diverse and constantly evolving process. Understanding both the aesthetic and technical use of color is key to effectively communicating the messages you create as a designer. The rest of this book examines the different aspects of color that will affect your work.

CHAPTER 2

Color Perception

Consumers make judgments within ninety seconds, and a large portion of those decisions are based on color. Color is one of the most strategic marketing tools at our disposal; it affects every industry from carpet to automotive to clothing to computers. It influences emotions, creates symbolic associations, reinforces brand identities, and enhances the perceived value of products.

Whether your product is a car, a vegetable, a candidate, or even an idea, the goal of all marketing — and ultimately, of graphic design — is to sell something. To effectively communicate your message — and in turn, sell the product — you need to have some understanding of how color is perceived and interpreted by consumers, and how the colors you use can influence purchasing decisions.

Color perception is influenced by psychological, biological, and environmental factors, and is at least partially the result of social conditioning that begins at an early age. As children we learn that red is hot (don't touch the fire on the stove), green is poison (Mr. Yuk stickers identify dangerous chemicals), and black is scary (there *are* monsters in the dark). A pink birthday card is for a girl, and a blue one is for a boy. These conditioned responses play a significant role in the way we interpret the color in graphic design.

Think of what each of these "colored" phrases refer to:

Green-eyed monster   White wedding   Blue-blooded

What colors come to mind when you think of the following concepts?

Warmth   Danger   Sickness

It is not our purpose here to tell you what colors to use in your design work. Rather, our goal is to explain the different ways that color can affect the consumer mind, which in turn can inform the choices you make in your designs.

The Metaphor of Color

A symbol is a visual metaphor, or a type of visual shorthand, that we tend to use interchangeably with an idea or concept. Symbolism is a visual language, and is an important aspect of graphic design. Color is the most abstract form of symbolism; it is by itself symbolic, and can also change the perceived meaning of a specific colored object.

As you learned in Chapter 1, color has long carried symbolic attachment; such symbolism was perhaps more prominent in preliterate cultures than it is today. As an example, the color of a medieval person's clothing often reflected his or her social status — the dyes used to produce certain colors of cloth were prohibitively expensive for all but the very wealthy. In some societies, it was even considered a crime to wear colors reserved for the royal and ruling classes.

Heraldry, the ritualized development of official family devices such as the identity crest shown below, is a highly artistic form of symbolism. Heraldic crests were used to establish identity, ownership, and heredity. In a medieval countryside, a person could easily and with certainty identify an approaching rider by the symbols and colors on the rider's crest. The art of heraldry made strong use of color (or *tincture*) to convey a person's family heritage. The different elements of the crest are of course symbolic, but so too are the colors of each element.

Color symbolism has both cultural and psychological significance. Although it is no longer a crime to wear the

If you have never studied medieval history, you probably wouldn't recognize this symbol of King James I of England.

Heraldic Color Meanings

Gold	Generosity and elevation of mind
Silver	Peace and sincerity
Red	Bravery, strength, generosity, and justice.
Blue	Truth and loyalty
Green	Hope, joy, and love
Black	Constancy or grief

wrong color, consider how many different conventions still dictate clothing color. We shouldn't wear white after Labor Day. We wear pastels for weddings, black for funerals. Wearing red or blue (in the United States) suggests political affiliation, loyalty, and patriotism — or it might be a symbol of gang activity. We usually wear light colors in the spring, darker tones in the fall. The list goes on...

The Emotion of Color

Understanding and effectively using color as a symbolic or motivational tool is key to effective visual communication. Rather than thinking of color symbolism as a limitation, you should use it to your advantage. When planning design for any medium, remember that the colors you use carry as much symbolic power as the specific objects of the design. Different colors cause or contribute to different emotional reactions, which can be powerful motivators in purchasing decisions.

There is a large body of literature devoted to the psychological meaning of different colors; it would be impossible to list every possible interpretation here. Rather, we aim to open your awareness to the different ways color choices may be perceived. It is also important to note two facts about color symbolism. First, most colors have a variety of possible — and often contradictory — meanings; you should be aware of the potential for suggesting the *opposite* meaning of what you originally intended. Second, colors may have different meanings in different cultures; here we discuss Euro-American interpretation; if you are designing for a specific cultural audience, you should investigate the potential interpretation for that specific culture.

SEEING RED

Red is the most obvious emotional color. It is used to suggest a wide range of emotions from love (a red rose or St. Valentine's Day) to anger (seeing red) to loyalty (red-blooded) to treachery (red coat). A red-carpet welcome usually precedes a grand and special event, and a particularly memorable event is considered a red-letter day. A red cross is the universal symbol of medical care, and the International Red Cross formalized the symbol as its organization logo.

Red also suggests power and vitality, and is attractive to people who place value on an intense experience. Many products use red packaging or red association to meet just that requirement. Red cars are fast (and in fact cost more to insure). Red meat provides a hearty and filling meal, and Red Bull energy drink promises to "give you wings."

Red, like other colors, has negative associations as well. If you're in debt, you're said to be "in the red." Government bureaucracy often requires wading through red tape. A red herring is a false or misleading clue. A red flag warns of danger, and a red-light district suggests the seedier side of town.

Different shades of red imply different meanings. For example, pink is now considered to be a little girl's color — although that wasn't always the case. In fact, prior to about the 1950s, pink was often considered a strong, intense color (as a version of red) and was preferred for little boys' clothing. Pink is also used to enhance the sense of sweetness, which is why bakery goods are often packaged in pink boxes. Pink suggests a greater value for goods or services packaged with the color (the proverbial "rose-tinted glasses" effect).

The color purple is historically associated with royalty because of the extraordinary expense involved in making purple dye. Before chemical dyes were invented, the only natural source of true purple dye was the Murex shellfish — dying a single garment purple required the painstaking collection of the secretions of tens of thousands of mollusks. Wearing purple clothing was sometimes forbidden to anyone outside the ruling class in some medieval cultures, although it was unlikely that many people could afford purple in any case. Purple is also associated with myth and fantasy; wizards walk around draped in purple cloaks, and monsters are often depicted in shades of purple. As a symbol of wisdom, purple is often linked to academia. Purple also promotes creativity, and is a favorite color for many artists.

FOLLOW THE YELLOW BRICK ROAD

Yellow — the sun — is a happy color that suggests spring and a feeling of newness. The 1960s gave us the eternal yellow happy-face symbol, emblazoned on everything from pajamas to bumper stickers. Tying a yellow ribbon 'round an oak tree was a symbol of hope, and the Yellow Brick Road leads to a magical place where wishes are fulfilled.

Because the human eye processes yellow faster than any other color, yellow is also a symbol of danger or caution. Yellow road signs warn that the road might be slippery, that deer may be crossing the road, or that pedestrians are lurking. Yellow is a natural warning symbol as a danger sign: yellow bees sting, yellow and black spiders bite, and yellow foliage might be poisonous.

Yellow is perceived as spontaneous, and is commonly associated with speed and gratification. Many companies that want to be associated with fast service use yellow as the predominant color in brand identity. Western Union's logo is yellow and black; you can send money anywhere quickly. Taxi cabs are yellow — fast transportation. Midas and Meineke, two national auto services, have yellow identities — fast service. The Yellow Pages is a reliable source to quickly find the information you need.

IT'S NOT EASY BEING GREEN

Green has been a symbol of nature for centuries, as far back as the Green Man (the nature god) in ancient Celtic culture. Grass, plants, trees, and other natural organisms are brilliant green when they are alive. Environmental groups like Greenpeace and the Green Party frequently use the green-nature symbolism in their advertising and even their names.

Green suggests freshness or new life, from which we get the expression that a new staff member or recruit is green. The symbolic link between green and nature tells us that green foods are good for us. They are healthy, fresh, full of nutrients, and all the things that are considered to be worth eating.

> When Erik The Red was exiled from Iceland (a perfectly unfriendly name for a country) for manslaughter in 982, he traveled to and settled the island we now know as Greenland. Historians and scientists argue that the climate then was different, which means that the island was, in fact, green. Legend, however, commonly holds that Erik named the arctic island "Greenland" to attract new settlers.

Green also often suggests sickness, at least partially because of social conditioning. For many years, hospitals, schools, and other public institutions were painted with muted shades of green because the cool color can have a calming effect. That trend now leads us to associate "hospital green" with sickness. Mr. Yuk, the well-known green frown from the Poison Control Center, has become a universal warning that something is dangerous or poisonous. If a person is ill, they may be "green around the gills" or just look a bit green.

In the United States, money is printed with green ink. Green has come to symbolize wealth (and the negative aspects of wealth, greed and jealousy). Other cultures may not have green money, but they are aware of this color symbolism. In fact, green as a symbol of jealousy long predates U.S. currency; Shakespeare warned to "beware, my lord, of jealousy; it is the green-ey'd monster..."

A CASE OF THE BLUES

From a biological perspective, the presence of blue causes the body to release endorphins, which make us feel better. Blue is a passive, tranquil color that is associated with contentment and security. Many companies in the health care and financial industries use blue as a predominant color in branding, as do companies that want to project the impression of reliability and longevity.

Blue is also considered to be a serious, professional color. A dark blue power suit announces that the wearer is serious about the business at hand. Medium shades of blue are frequently used as backgrounds for political figures to enhance their image of veracity, conservative values, honesty, and steadfastness. The term "blue-blood" has long been used to imply loyalty and patriotism.

Following the theme of contradictory color symbolism, blue has also been associated with sadness and depression since the Elizabethan age. In the musical sense, the Blues — the music genre that evolved from music traditions in the American slave population — tell stories of profound despair, sorrow, and loss. Blue also symbolizes victory ("blue-ribbon recipe"), rarity ("once in a blue moon"), high value ("blue-chip stock"), and puritanical beliefs ("blue laws").

WHITE AS A GHOST

White, the sum of all colors, most commonly represents purity or cleanliness. White suggests unblemished purity — an immaculate canvas or a starched shirt; goodness — the good guy always wears white; and innocence — before anything has sullied the pure white.

Like most colors, white symbolism can also be contradictory. White represents the void, or a lack of anything at all. The arctic tundra, a barren and uninhabitable expanse of land, is perceived as white (even though in reality the tundra actually has a short growing season with mild summer temperatures every year). The Ice Queen from childhood fairy tales is another example of white's negative symbolism. White, in this case, suggests bitterness, meanness, relentlessness. Jack Frost, another fictional character usually portrayed in white, suggests coldness and hardness.

A white-collar profession does not require manual labor, and is therefore preferable to the more strenuous blue-collar labor. A white flag signals surrender, and white-washing suggests that facts are being concealed. A white elephant no longer has value for the owner, yet white meat is perceived to be healthier than red meat.

BLACK AS PITCH

We know that the guy in a black shirt and black cowboy hat is not the good guy, and Death personified (the Grim Reaper) appears in a voluminous black cloak. Witches wear black, have black cats, and practice black magic; black widows are very poisonous spiders. Blackbeard, the Black Knight, and Black Bart are just a few examples of black's notorious association with historical "blackguards." Black food is often rotten or poisonous. In western cultures, we wear black to funerals and hang a black wreath on the door; the Black Plague was one of the worst ever to devastate Europe.

The expression "black sheep of the family" originated in agricultural cultures, where black wool brought a far lower price at market because it could not be dyed; thus, the black sheep were undesirable. If a person is blackballed or blacklisted, he or she is no longer welcome among a group of peers. The Black Market is an underground channel for acquiring illegal goods and services. The term "black hole" is used to describe a void or emptiness.

Contradicting the negative symbolism, black also suggests sophistication, elegance, and wealth. We attend black-tie events in black gowns and tuxedos, driven in black limousines. Expensive luxury products such as chocolate and caviar are often packaged in black wrapping, and black is a popular color for most luxury cars.

SHADES OF GRAY

Would you even consider buying a black-and-white television? Probably not. But in the design world, black and white can be just as powerful as full color. Black-and-white images don't need to look like they were produced on an old copy machine. A more appropriate term to describe black-and-white design is "grayscale," which indicates that shades of gray are used to reproduce images.

Since color reproduction became possible for mainstream media — including print, television, and film — anything that could be in color was. Color televisions went on sale in the United States in 1951, and media advertising almost universally switched to full color. Black-and-white images quickly became an indication of something old fashioned, cheap, or out-of-date.

Recently, however, grayscale graphics have become more popular as alternatives to brilliant, screaming color. Using grayscale conveys a very specific message — nostalgic, classic, "retro" (interestingly this still means "old-fashioned," but now it's acceptable), and distinguished. Think of the products that use black-and-white television and magazine ads — perfume, jewelry, luxury cars. Companies such as DeBeers and Mercedes use black-and-white television and print advertising to suggest sophistication. The use of grayscale also suggests tradition — Mercedes has been around for a long time.

Selective Color

Modern film and television productions have made effective use of black and white as a powerful symbolic tool. The movie *Pleasantville* (Larger than Life Productions and New Line Cinema, 1998) tells the story of the "perfect" black-and-white 1950s-like world in which a culturally isolated community is exposed to emotional and social uncertainty. The beginning of the movie is filmed entirely in black and white; as the townspeople embrace such concepts as "silly" and "sexy," more objects and people in the town become "colored."

As the story progresses, the town conservatives meet to discuss how things can go back to the way they once were. Signs in store windows proclaim "No Coloreds" — drawing a direct comparison to the racial segregation that would have almost certainly been present in a 1950s town like Pleasantville. The presence of color, in this case, is a creative approach to a discussion of integration; color as an element is also a symbol of change and enlightenment.

Schindler's List (Amblin Entertainment and Universal Pictures, 1993) provides another example of how color can be used to tell an unspoken story. The movie is filmed almost entirely in black and white. The movie's topic, the Holocaust, is poignantly underlined by the appearance of a single object in color throughout the entire three hours and seven minutes. A young Jewish girl wearing a red coat appears in the opening scenes; the red coat is later visible in a pile of clothes taken from those who were or would be killed.

The Flavor of Color

For product marketing, especially food products, color is more important than just a pretty package. The psychological reaction to color influences many of our purchases, both positive and negative. If the color of food appears "off," we believe that it won't taste right either.

In many cases, color is a gauge of freshness. We judge individual pieces of fruit or vegetables, passing off the pale ones as unripe, and very dark ones as overripe. A bright red hot-house tomato in February is perceived to be better than a pinkish one, even though both can be equally flavorful or flavorless.

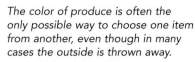

The color of produce is often the only possible way to choose one item from another, even though in many cases the outside is thrown away.

If an orange appears too yellow, people won't buy it. In fact, some orange growers add dye to ripe oranges before sending them to the consumer market. The bright, vibrant color we expect to see in a ripe orange could be the result of a carefully researched strategy based on human color perception.

There is a large body of research devoted to finding the "right" color for a specific food. An researcher in the early 1970s served people a meal of steak and french fries that appeared normal beneath colored lights. According to Eric Schlosser, "Everyone thought the meal tasted fine until the lighting was changed. Once it became apparent that the steak was actually blue and the fries were green, some people became ill" (*Fast Food Nation*, Perennial Books, 2001).

MEMORY COLOR

The idea of specific foods being certain colors extends far beyond the produce department. Many things in our world are specific colors; the sky is blue, grass is green, fire trucks are (usually) red. We generally have a preconceived notion of the "correct" color of certain objects. This perceptual phenomenon is called *memory color*, or the tendency to evaluate color based on what we expect to see rather than what is actually there.

Although this image is reproduced only in black ink, your subconscious memory provides the color.

Ketchup is red because we expect tomato products to be red. Heinz recently introduced "funky" green-, purple-, and blue colored ketchup to increase the appeal to a youthful audience.

When we look at images, we generally compare the appearance of the image content to what we believe to be true. If an object is produced in some other color, or if the color's brightness and saturation are not as expected, the object will not seem quite right. This can be used to your advantage — wouldn't you stop and take notice of a park with purple grass? People are drawn to anything that strays from their expectations.

THE ALL-NATURAL INFLUENCE

In most cases, we prefer to consume foods that appear to be in their natural states. Most of the adults we know wrinkle their noses a little at the thought of blue ketchup or purple milk — those products just don't seem quite right. In reality, though, most of the foods that make up the typical American diet have undergone a great deal of processing and refinement, but we just don't realize it. Milk is typically processed —

Many natural (that is, less processed) food selections are now available at supermarkets. Even unbleached coffee filters are available — the implication is that unbleached filters will brew healthier coffee than standard white, bleached filters. Of course, coffee made with brown filters will have no less caffeine, and the filters are still made using all the requisite chemicals for paper making; the only real difference is that no bleach is used to alter the paper's "natural" color.

pasteurized and homogenized — before we drink it. Sugar, flour, and rice are highly processed and bleached before reaching the market. We have come to believe that these products are naturally white, although in their natural states they are actually various shades of brown.

The recent cultural emphasis placed on natural food products has begun to change the content and layout of grocery-store shelves. Raw brown sugar crystals, unbleached (or even whole wheat) flour, brown rice, and a host of other "natural" products are available as more "healthy" alternatives to the traditionally refined white products. Food marketers recognize that many people use the brown coloring to gauge the apparent healthiness of food selections, of course, so they sometimes add "caramel coloring" to simulate the appearance of more natural ingredients.

PACKAGING AND BRAND IDENTITY

One of the goals of packaging design is to *create* a memory color. Color is a very effective branding tool, as important as layout for many companies. If you see a Coca-Cola can on a black-and-white television, you still know what color it is. Color is so important to Coca-Cola that the company holds a copyright on that particular red ink. Successful corporate brand design relies on the ability to plant the company's image in the consumer mind as easily recognizable symbols, even when they are abstracted to the most basic element.

Tomato products are packaged in bright red because fresh tomatoes are expected to be bright red. Orange juice is almost always packaged in bright orange containers, even if the juice in the package appears more yellow than orange. Cleaning products are often packaged in white or blue because we associate those colors with cleanliness. In many cases, the color of the packaging is more appetizing than the product itself; but purchasing decisions are based on packaging.

Many products are so closely associated with the color of packaging that the products become synonymous with the color.

Because green is perceived as fresh and natural, a wealth of cleaning products are also artificially colored and packaged in shades of green. The green color of Irish Spring soap will make you feel like you just stepped out of a fresh mountain stream. Of course, that mountain stream may be terribly polluted, but the important point is the psychological association between a natural green environment and a green bar of soap.

Exactly how clean is an Irish spring?

COMPLEMENTARY COLORS

Complementary color means opposite colors on the color wheel (explained in Chapter 3). Using complementary colors in a design can enhance and strengthen the appearance of what you are trying to highlight, which is especially useful for point-of-purchase and packaging design. Red apples are displayed in green or blue casing, and bags of carrots frequently have blue or purple lettering. The complementary colors make the produce look brighter, which leads people to think it is fresher.

Surrounding colors can change the way we perceive an object. Complementary colors are commonly used to enhance the appearance of a product.

The Business of Color

Color is so important to marketing that, in many cases, color language is strong enough to identify a company. How many of these slogans or catch phrases do you recognize?

Golden arches

Get blue

What can brown do for you?

I've got the blues

The little purple pill

The other white meat

Get PINK

Almost everyone will recognize that the golden arches are synonymous with McDonald's. Some are more recognizable than others; some are recent introductions while others have survived decades. The remaining products or companies are:

- **Get blue.** Introduced in 2001, American Express offers a consumer-level credit card. The card is blue with a hologram on it, and looks very different from the traditional green American Express card.
- **What can brown do for you?** UPS's recognizable brown trucks have given birth to the company's latest and largest advertising campaign, aimed at expanding the customer base to compete with similar delivery services and the United States Post Office.
- **I've got the blues.** Kraft Macaroni and Cheese, one of the packages we referred to when discussing memory color, takes the box color a step further with this colored slogan.
- **The little purple pill.** Using television to advertise pharmaceuticals is a controversial topic, but AstraZeneca Pharmaceuticals realized that "The Little Purple Pill" is friendlier and easier to remember than the proper name of the drug (Nexium).
- **The other white meat.** The National Pork Board launched this campaign in 1987, partially in response to the growing awareness that red meat contributes to high cholesterol. The slogan positioned pork as a healthier alternative to beef at every dinner, although it is technically still a "red" meat.
- **Get PINK.** In the 1980s, Owens Corning connected the color of it's main consumer product — fiber glass insulation — to the Pink Panther cartoon. By 1990, the company found that consumers chose PINK insulation products five times more than the competition.

THE BONDI REVOLUTION

In 1998, Apple Computer used a simple concept to forever change its corporate image — they added color. The consumer-level iMac in Bondi blue added a bright spot to many otherwise beige desks. The following year, a rainbow of fruit-flavored iMacs — Grape, Tangerine, Lime, Blueberry, and Strawberry — appeared on the market. (Interestingly, the well-known rainbow of Apple's company logo abandoned color in favor of solid white.)

Shortly after Apple colored our office worlds, retail markets were flooded with a range of products available in bright, translucent plastics that allowed us to color-coordinate our cell phones, televisions, computers, and toasters.

The colorful iMac (helped, in large part, by its comparatively low price) gave Apple the power necessary to reach a consumer market that had been overwhelmingly Windows-based. In fact, Windows-based computer manufacturers quickly followed Apple's challenge with their own colorful desktop models.

MELTS IN YOUR MOUTH, NOT IN YOUR HAND

One of the most popular candies in the world provides an excellent example of how color can be both a brand identity and a marketing tool. First sold in 1941, M&Ms were originally a single brown color. Red, green, and yellow were added to the mix in 1960 when peanut M&Ms were introduced, and orange was added in 1976.

Also in 1976, red M&Ms were removed due to public controversy surrounding a specific red food coloring. The specific coloring agent in question was never used in the candies, but was removed anyway to avoid public confusion. Red was added back into the blend in 1987 as a result of overwhelming requests from consumers.

M&Ms packages are closely monitored to contain the right mix of colors:

30% Brown	10% Blue
20% Yellow	10% Orange
20% Red	10% Green

In 1995, a huge marketing event asked Americans to vote for a new color — blue, pink, purple, or no change — to appear in the M&Ms mix. Blue won by a landslide with 54% of the more than 10 million votes cast.

In 2002, the company launched the Global Color Vote advertising campaign for consumers to choose between pink, purple, and aqua. The campaign attracted more than 10 million votes from over 200 countries. Of the three choices, purple pulled in 41% of the vote; aqua was a close second with 37%, and pink got only 19%.

Conclusion

We could easily write an entire book listing all the distinct examples of color in advertising and corporate identity — which suggests exactly how important color really is. There are also countless examples of the symbolic meanings of color; we have discussed many of those meanings here, but you shouldn't think that this chapter is exhaustive.

To successfully communicate your message, you need to first select the appropriate colors for the job, then create them appropriately for the media you are using. In this chapter we discussed how human color perception influences your color choices. The remaining chapters of the book will examine the issues and techniques important to reproducing the colors you choose.

CHAPTER 3

Color Theory

Regardless of your output goal, you cannot accurately reproduce color without a basic understanding of color theory. Keep in mind that we say *basic* — color theory is a complex, often confusing topic. The following discussion presents the issues that will help you to understand and effectively use color in design.

In the most basic sense, color is light. Different wavelengths of light are visualized as different colors. The human visual system can detect light waves between 400 and 700 nanometers (nm) in length, which make up the *visible spectrum* or range of visible colors. Light waves below 400 nm (including ultraviolet) and above 700 (including infrared) are not discernible by the human eye.

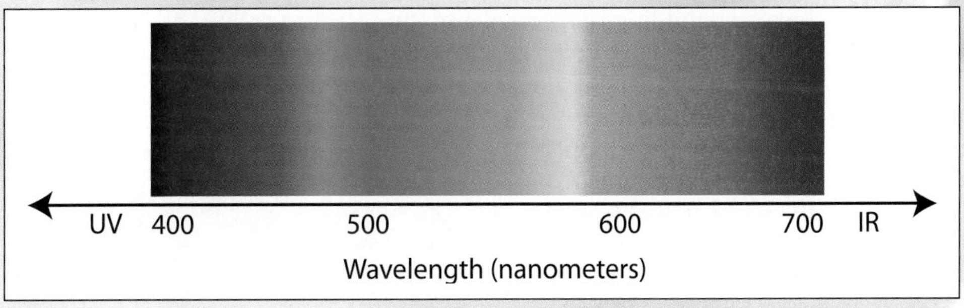

Additive Color

The additive color model is based on the idea that all colors can be reproduced by combining pure red, green, and blue light in varying intensities. These three colors are considered the *additive primaries*, and are the basis of most digital color reproduction (used by televisions, computer monitors, digital cameras, and scanners).

Although usually considered a "color," black is the absence of light (and, therefore, of color). Combining any two additive primaries at full strength produces one of the *additive secondaries* — red and blue light combine to produce magenta, red and green combine to produce yellow, and blue and green combine to produce cyan. White is the sum of all colors, produced when all three additive primaries are combined at full strength.

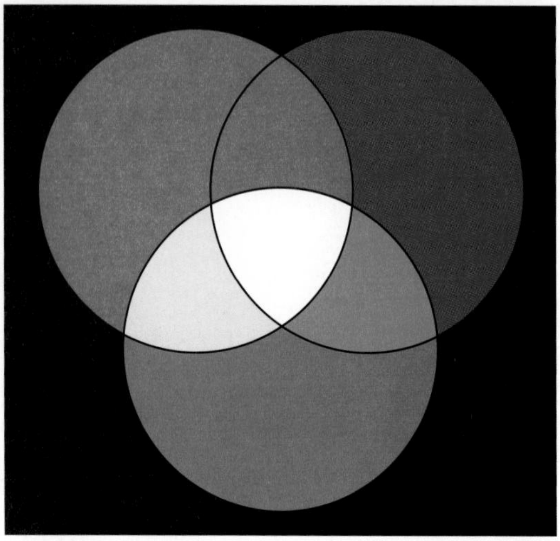

The additive color model.

Additive color theory is practically applied when a reproduction method uses light to reproduce color. A television screen or computer monitor is black when it is turned off. When the power is turned on, light in the monitor illuminates at different intensities to create the range of colors you see.

Subtractive Color

Printing pigmented inks on a substrate, of course, is a very different method of reproducing color — it does not begin with a black screen, and it does not involve a source of light. Reproducing color on paper requires *subtractive color theory*, which is essentially the inverse of additive color theory.

Instead of adding red, green, and blue light to create the range of colors, subtractive color begins with a white surface that reflects red, green, and blue light at equal and full strength. To reflect a specific color, a surface must subtract or absorb only certain wavelengths from the white light. To reflect only red, for example, the surface must subtract (or absorb) the green and blue light.

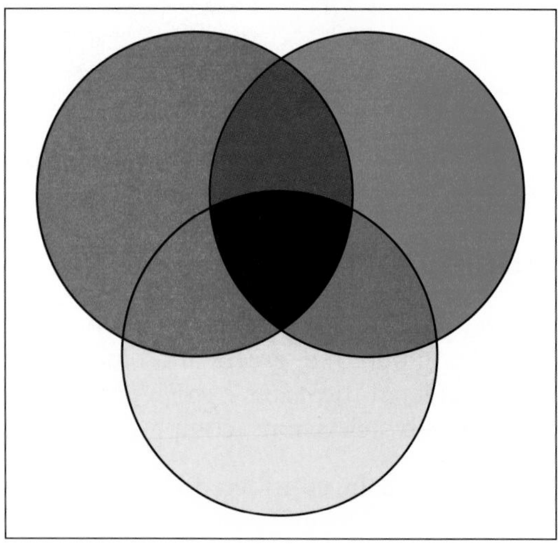

The subtractive color model.

Remember that the additive primary colors (red, green, and blue) combine to create the additive secondaries (cyan, magenta, and yellow). Those additive secondaries are also called the "subtractive primaries," because each subtracts one-third of the light spectrum, and reflects the other two thirds:

- Cyan absorbs red light, reflecting only blue and green light.
- Magenta absorbs green light, reflecting only red and blue light.
- Yellow absorbs blue light, reflecting only red and green light.

A combination of two subtractive primaries, then, absorbs two-thirds of the light spectrum and reflects only one-third. As an example, a combination of yellow and magenta absorbs both blue and green light, reflecting only red.

> Understand the relationship between additive and subtractive primaries:
>
> | | |
> |---|---|
> | Cyan = Minus Red | (RGB – R = C) |
> | Magenta = Minus Green | (RGB – G = M) |
> | Yellow = Minus Blue | (RGB – B = Y) |

We mentioned earlier that red and green light combine to make yellow. According to additive color theory, yellow is the result of the absence of blue light. Using subtractive color theory, yellow reflects red and green light and absorbs blue; as a subtractive primary, yellow is sometimes referred to as "minus blue" (RGB – B = Y).

To practically apply subtractive color theory (as in color printing), inks made with cyan, magenta, and yellow pigments are combined to absorb different wavelengths of light. To create the appearance of red, the green and blue light must be subtracted or absorbed, thus reflecting only red. Magenta absorbs green light, and yellow absorbs blue light; combining magenta and yellow inks on white paper reflects only the red light. By combining different amounts of the subtractive primaries, it's possible to produce a large range or *gamut* of colors.

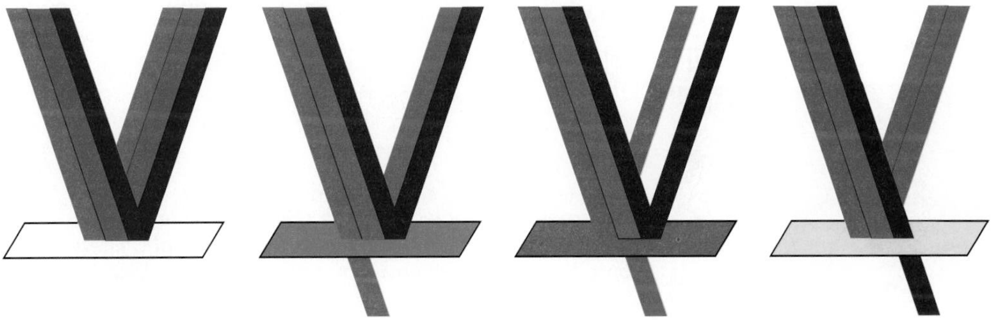

Understanding Complementary Color

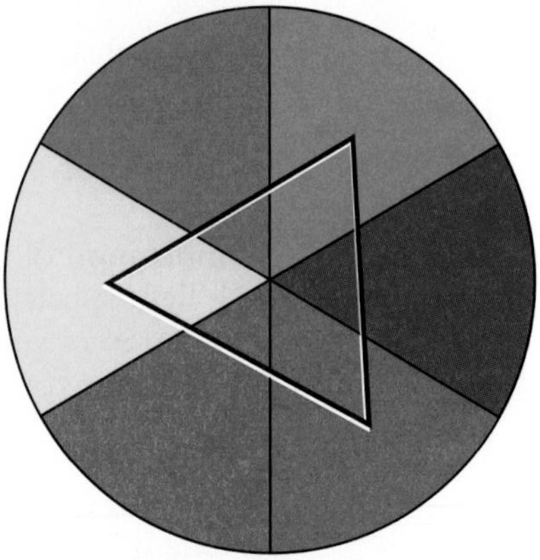

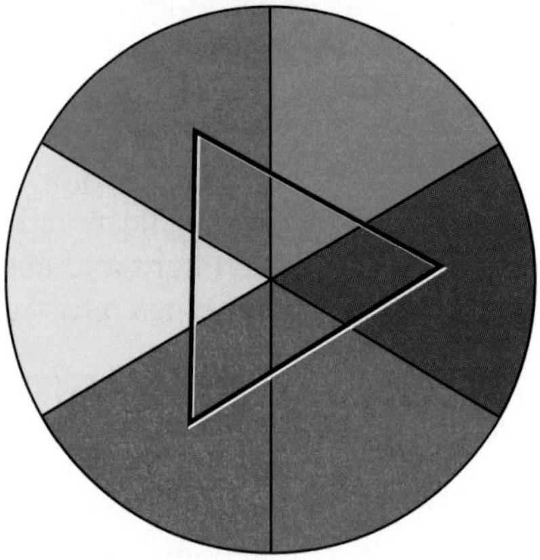

If you place an equilateral triangle over the color wheel, the three points indicate either the RGB or CMY primary colors. The line that connects each point in the triangle indicates the result of mixing those primaries.

A basic color wheel is helpful to understand the concept of additive and subtractive color theory. As the colors are positioned on a color wheel, red, green, and blue (collectively called the "RGB colors") are directly inverse (opposite) to cyan, magenta, and yellow (called the "CMY colors").

Referencing the color wheel allows us to understand how RGB colors relate to CMY colors. If you center an equilateral triangle over the color wheel, the points of the triangle touch either the RGB primaries or the CMY primaries. Adding together two points of the triangle results in the color between the two points. Red and blue combine to form magenta, yellow and cyan combine to form green, and so on. This is why the two color modes are said to be "directly inverse." Each CMY color is made up of two RGB colors and vice versa.

Opposite colors on the color wheel are called *color complements*. Using subtractive color theory, a color's complement absorbs or subtracts that color from visible white light. As an example, cyan is opposite

Photographing an object through cyan (bottom left), magenta (bottom middle), and yellow (bottom right) filters shows the effects of removing the red, green, and blue wavelengths of light.

red on the color wheel; cyan absorbs red light and reflects green and blue. Because you know green and blue light combine to create cyan, you can begin to understand how the two theories are related.

Obviously, a red apple is not red because only red light is shining. It is red because the surface absorbs green and blue light and reflects red light. Cyan is red's complement — it absorbs red light. Placing a cyan filter over a red apple removes the red color. The same concept applies to items of different colors.

Human Color Perception

The most important thing to remember about color theory is that color is light, and light is color. You can easily prove this by walking through your house at midnight; you will notice (after your shins stop throbbing from bumping into the coffee table) that what little you can see appears as dark shadows.

Without light, you can't see — and without light, there is no color.

The biology of color vision is the heart of color perception. Because this is not a science book, we present here a very simplified explanation of color vision and human color perception.

Light enters the eye through the lens and is focused on the retina. In the retina, a group of tiny cells called rods and cones (collectively referred to as "photoreceptors") respond to the light; these cells stimulate special nerve cells, which pass on signals to the brain.

Rods are not sensitive to color; they capture lightness information, and work best in low-light conditions. Rods allow you to determine how much light there is, but not the color of the light.

Cones are the color receivers of the human eye. They are concentrated at the center of the retina, where the visual field is most focused. Cones contain a photopigment called "rhodopsin," which stimulates an electrochemical response to light. There are three different types of rhodopsin; one absorbs shorter wavelengths of light, one absorbs medium wavelengths, and one absorbs longer wavelengths.

There are several different forms of abnormal color vision or color blindness, which is a genetic defect usually passed on the X chromosome. Research suggests that approximately 5–8% of all men and 0.5–1% of women have some form of abnormal color vision.

The most common abnormality is *anomalous trichromacy*, characterized by a shift in the sensitivity to one or more wavelength ranges. The inability to distinguish between red and green is the most common, least severe form of anomalous trichromacy; many affected people are unaware of their deficiency.

Dichromacy, or the lack of one of the three types of cone receptors, is a less common form of abnormal color vision.

Monochromacy is a third (and extremely rare) type of abnormal color vision; it results in an entire lack of color vision.

Abnormal color vision is obviously a problem for anyone who has to make color judgments, including graphic designers and printing professionals. Some companies require applicants to take a color vision test before they can be hired.

We perceive specific colors because the pigments in an object's surface absorb different wavelengths of light (called "spectral absorption"), reflecting only the wavelengths that define the object's color (called "spectral reflectance"). As an example, a lemon's surface absorbs blue light, reflecting red and green wavelengths to create the visual appearance of yellow.

The surface characteristics of an object absorb and reflect varying percentages of the different wavelengths. Because white is a combination of all colors, white paper should theoretically reflect equal percentages of all light wavelengths. However, different papers may absorb or reflect varying percentages of some wavelengths, thus defining the paper's apparent color. The paper's color will affect the appearance of ink color printed on that paper.

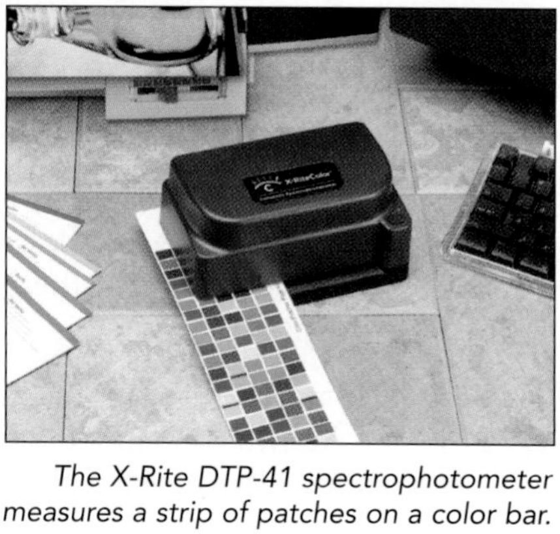

The X-Rite DTP-41 spectrophotometer measures a strip of patches on a color bar.

A *spectrophotometer* is used to precisely measure the wavelengths that are reflected from an object's surface, whether that object is a natural object, a printed page, or a blank piece of paper.

How Lighting Affects Color

Additive color supposes that the three colors of light — red, green, and blue — are added to a black space — the lack of light — to create all the colors in the visible spectrum. According to subtractive color theory, cyan, magenta, and yellow pigments subtract the red, green, and blue components of pure white light to create the colors in the visible spectrum. The practical application of these theories, however, is not so simple.

The light source in any particular viewing situation can (sometimes dramatically) affect the perceived color of an object. "White" light is rarely pure white — each of the three primaries combined at full strength. The color of a specific light source can add a *color cast* to a design, and can cause the same color to appear different under various lighting conditions (called "metamerism").

The term "color temperature" is used to define the color properties of a light source. As an object is heated it first glows red, then yellow, then white, then blue. Cooler color temperatures, correspondingly, have a yellow cast and the hottest color temperature has a blue cast.

2000K — Candlelight

2750K — Incandescent Light

3000K — Tungsten Light
Warm Fluorescent Light

4100K — Cool Fluorescent Light

5000K — Graphic Arts Viewing Standard

6000K — Noon Sun

12000K — Noon Sky

> Color temperature is measured on the Kelvin (K) scale, in which 0K — absolute zero — is the coldest possible temperature, equivalent to –273°C. Note that no degree symbol is used with the Kelvin temperature scale.

Lighting conditions can case images to have an overall color cast.

It is interesting to note that physical color temperature is contradictory to human color perception; we perceive yellow hues as "warm" and blues as "cool."

Fluorescent light, commonly used in office settings, ranges from 3000 to 4100K and often has a slight yellow or blue cast. Tungsten lights, which are commonly used in household lighting, have a color temperature around 3000K and a pronounced yellow cast. The graphic-arts industry uses 5000K light in controlled environments — press rooms, proofing stations, and so on — to allow production staff to match colors created in the design phase. This high temperature corresponds to white light with equal amounts of red, green, and blue light — and no cast — for optimum color viewing conditions.

As a designer, it is equally (if not more) important to consider the lighting conditions in which your final design will be viewed. If your product will be displayed under the fluorescent lights of a grocery store, you need to consider how the colors will look in those lighting conditions instead of in a controlled production environment.

If a light source has an apparent color cast, it means red, green, and blue wavelengths of light are not equal. Yellow light, for example, has stronger components of red and green and a weaker blue component.

Consider what would happen to a blue poster displayed under yellow lighting. The blue poster would be created from inks of cyan (to absorb red light) and magenta (to absorb green light), thus reflecting only blue light wavelengths. The yellow light source, though, would have only a weak blue component. The pigments used to create the blue poster would still absorb the red and green wavelengths from the light; the weaker blue wavelengths would be reflected, but not as brilliantly as if all three wavelengths were equally present.

Such a blue sign displayed in yellow light, then, would appear more grayish-black than blue. Although standardized viewing conditions are essential for matching design colors on a printing press, understanding the practical use and display of your work is essential to creating compelling color design.

Communicating Color

The language of color can be confusing, which makes it extremely difficult to communicate specific color concepts. You can tell someone to use a "nice, dark red," but what exactly is dark? And who decides what's "nice"?

To further confuse matters, different color terms can have similar meanings or a single term can have different meanings. These terms might also have different meanings depending on the speaker. Your clients might say something vague such as, "Make that brighter" when they really want a color to be more saturated. Or you may hear something like, "Make that greener." Unfortunately, we do not have a "Greener" button on most of our equipment, so we need to be able to translate our clients' statements about color into something physically meaningful.

Many vague and technical-sounding terms are mentioned when discussing color. Is hue the same as color? the same as value? the same as tone? What is the difference between lightness and brightness? What is chroma? And where does saturation fit in?

This problem has resulted in several attempts to normalize color communication. A number of *color systems* have been developed to define color according to specific criteria, including Hue, Saturation, and Brightness (HSB); Hue, Saturation, and Lightness (HSL); Hue, Saturation, and Value (HSV); and Lightness, Chroma, and Hue (LCH). Each of these models or systems plots color on a three-dimensional diagram, based on the elements of human color perception — hue, colorfulness, and brightness.

UNDERSTANDING THE TERMS

Hue is what most people think of as color — red, green, purple, and so on. Hue is defined according to a color's position on a color wheel, beginning from red (0°) and traveling counterclockwise around the wheel.

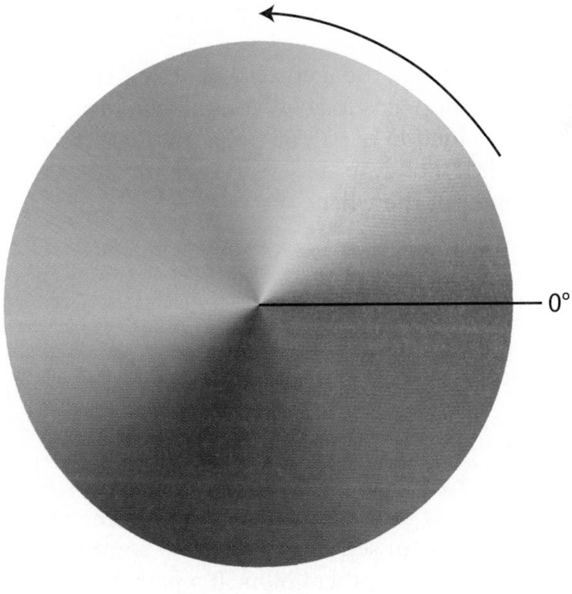

Hue is plotted around a color wheel. A color's hue angle is determined by measuring its distance in degrees from 0 (red).

Saturation (also called "intensity") refers to the color's difference from neutral gray. Highly saturated colors are more vivid than those with low saturation. Saturation is plotted on a color-space diagram from the center of the color wheel. Color at the center of the wheel is neutral gray, and has a saturation value of 0; a color at the edge of the wheel has a saturation value of 100, and is the most intense value of the corresponding hue.

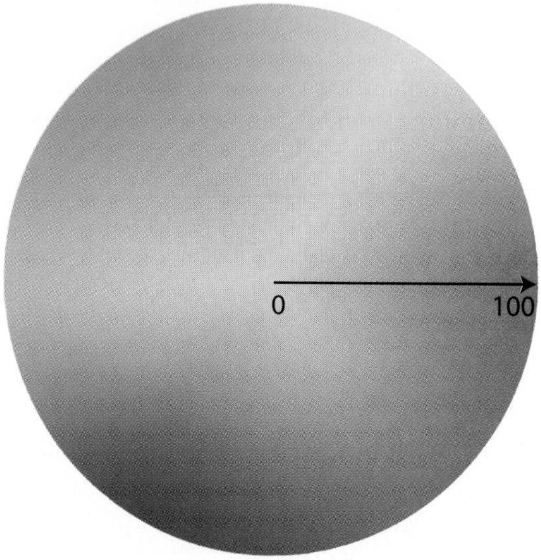

Colors on the outside of the color wheel have greater saturation or intensity.

If you bisect the color wheel with a straight line, the line makes up a saturation axis for two complementary colors. A color is dulled by the introduction of its complement. Red, for example, is neutralized by the addition of cyan (blue and green). As the two colors mix near the center of the wheel, the result is a neutral gray.

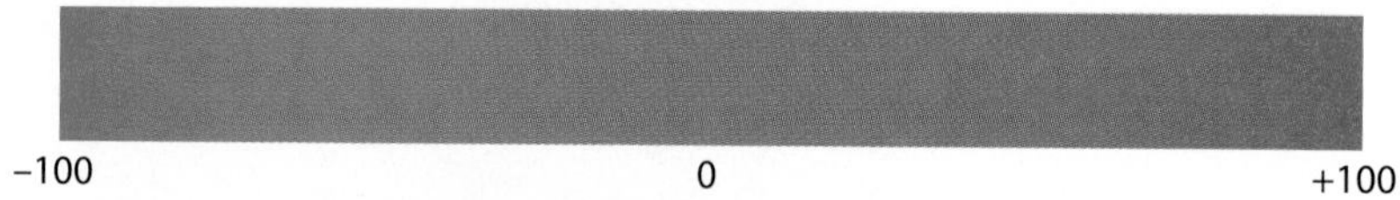

Chroma is similar to saturation, but factors in a reference white. In any viewing situation, colors appear less vivid when the light source dims. The process of *chromatic adaptation*, however, allows the human visual system to adjust to changes in light and still differentiate colors according to the relative saturation. The white area of a printed page, for example, can serve as a reference point from which to adjust one's perception of other colors. If a particular viewing situation does not have an identifiable white point for reference — such as dusk in a forest — then saturation is a better measure of colorfulness than chroma.

Brightness is the amount of light that is reflected. As an element of color reproduction, brightness is typically judged by comparing the color to the lightest nearby object (such as an unprinted area of white paper). It is important to note that there are many different variations of "white" paper, from the pristine coated paper used to print inkjet photos to the off-white newsprint used to print many books and daily papers; these variations affect the relative appearance of color brightness.

Lightness is the amount of white or black added to the pure color. Lightness (also called "luminance" or "value") is the relative brightness based purely on the black-white value of a color. In other words, lightness defines how light or dark a color is without regard to the specific color being described. A lightness of 0 means there is no addition of white or black. Lightness of +100 is pure white; lightness of –100 is pure black.

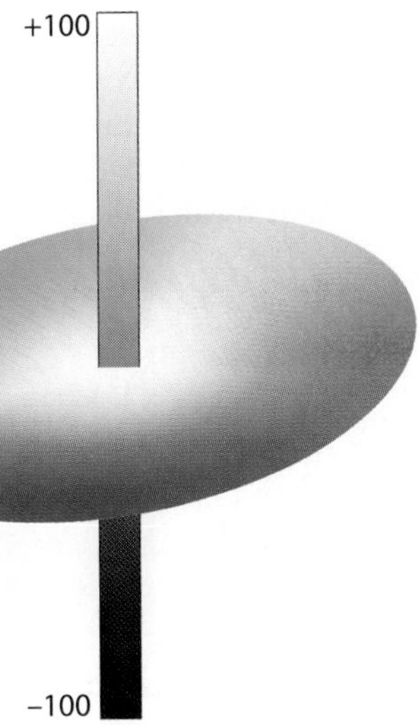

Lightness or brightness is defined as the blackness or whiteness of a color. Any specific hue around the color wheel is affected by the same lightness scale.

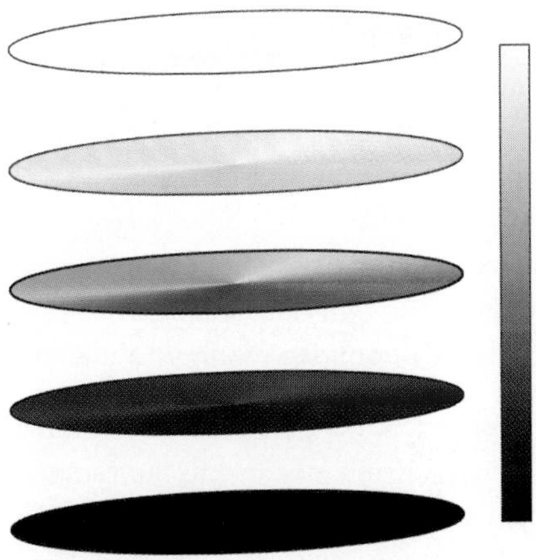

All hues are affected equally by changes in lightness.

Output Color Models

Most software applications allow you to choose from built-in color libraries, or to define new colors using several different *color models* or *color spaces*. The color model or space defines the structure of the color, or how the color will be created. Two primary color spaces are used to reproduce color — RGB color space and CMYK color space. Other color spaces or models are used to describe and communicate color, but those models are not "output" models because they do not specifically create the color you see on a monitor or a piece of paper.

RGB COLOR

The RGB color space is used in any device that reproduces color with light, such as televisions and computer monitors. The RGB color space reproduces the range of color according to additive color theory — red, green, and blue light are combined in varying intensities to create any color in the visible spectrum. Each color or *channel* in the RGB output model has 256 possible intensities (0–255).

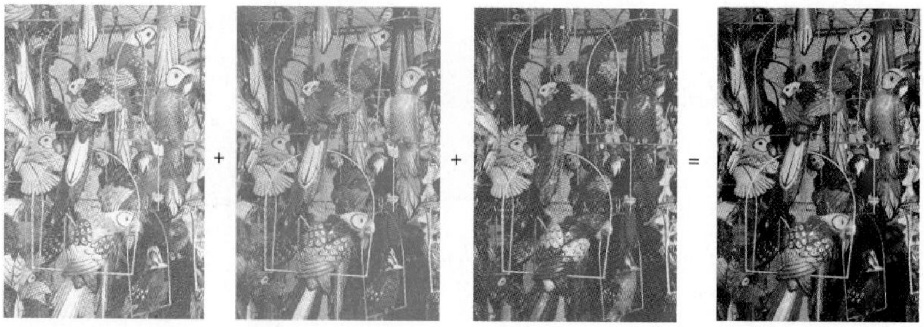

A number of factors can affect the appearance of color on an RGB output device. The internal mechanics used to create the red, green, and blue channels vary from one device to another. Different types of devices use various technologies, such as cathode ray tubes (CRTs)

Web-Safe Color

Computer monitors display in the RGB color model, so documents and images created for Web sites are created using RGB color. All computer monitors, however, display color somewhat differently — phosphorescence, monitor resolution, and other factors can affect how color is presented. For this reason, if you want your Web pages to look the same to everyone who accesses them, it is important to use only *Web-safe colors* to display color consistently from one monitor to the next.

Web-safe colors are specific RGB combinations that are most likely to appear the same (or close to the same) on most monitors on any platform. Applications that can be used for Web and multimedia design usually include libraries or palettes of predefined Web-safe colors, listed by hexadecimal value or name.

and light-emitting diodes (LEDs). The accuracy of a device's light source can deteriorate over time. The color of external light — such as the lamp in your office — can change the perceived color on the monitor. Because of these and other factors, RGB color is considered to be a *device-dependent* color model — the specific output device being used determines the final appearance of the color.

CMYK COLOR

The CMYK color model, also called "process color," uses subtractive color theory to reproduce the range of printable colors. The process-color model recreates the range of printable colors by overlapping layers of cyan, magenta, yellow, and black inks in varying percentages from 0–100.

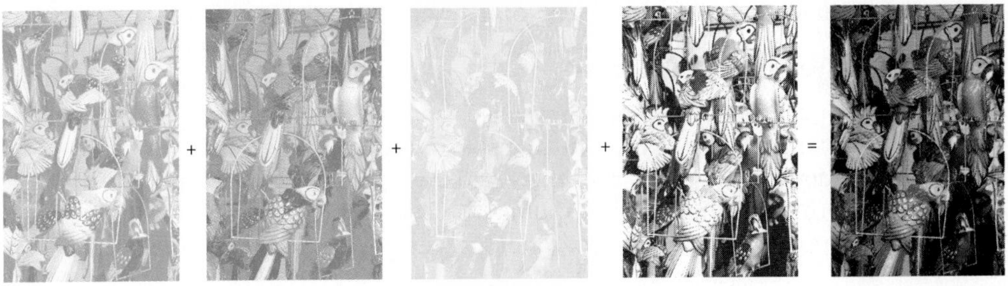

Using theoretically pure pigments, a mixture of equal parts of cyan, magenta, and yellow would produce black. Real pigments, however, are not pure; the actual result of mixing these three colors usually appears as a muddy brown.

The left block is printed with 100% black ink. The right block is a combination of 100% cyan, 100% magenta, and 100% yellow inks.

The fourth color, black (K), is added to the three subtractive primaries to extend the range of printable colors, and to allow much purer blacks to be printed than is possible with only the three primaries. Black is abbreviated as "K" because it is the "key" color to which others are aligned on the printing press. This also avoids confusion with blue in the RGB color model.

Like the RGB model, different factors can affect the appearance of any given CMYK build. The specific pigments used to make the inks, the color of paper on which a job is printed, and the color-reproduction characteristics of the press used can all affect the color that finally appears on the page. Because of this potential for difference, CMYK is also considered a device-dependent model. Color management, which we discuss in Chapter 6, addresses the problems associated with working in device-dependent color models.

Hexachrome Color

Hexachrome (also called "hifi" or "high-fidelity color") is the latest innovation in color printing. Standard printing presses have four printing units, one for each of the four primary CMYK inks; many of the new commercial printing presses, however (especially in the U.S.), have six or more printing units. The Hexachrome system, created by PANTONE, takes advantage of the additional printing units by adding two extra colors — green and orange — to the standard CMYK ink set. The green and orange units extend the color gamut so more shades can be reproduced on a traditional printing press.

Special Color Libraries

Special colors, commonly called "spot colors," are those that use a premixed ink to reproduce a specific color with a single ink layer — they are not built from the standard process inks used in CMYK printing. When you output a job with spot colors, each spot color appears on its own separation.

Spot-color inks are used in two- and three-color documents, and may be added to process-color documents when a special color, such as a corporate color, is needed. In the United States, the most popular collections of spot colors are the PANTONE Matching System (PMS) libraries. TruMatch and Focoltone are also used in the U.S.; Toyo and DICColor (Dainippon Ink & Chemicals) are used primarily in Japan.

Special inks exist because many of the colors cannot be reproduced with process inks (in the CMYK color space), nor can they be accurately represented on a computer monitor (in the RGB color space). Although most graphics applications include on-screen simulations of the most popular special-color libraries, you should look at a swatch book to select a particular color instead of selecting a color directly from the electronic library. Furthermore, if you specify a special color in a document, but then convert it to a CMYK process color, your job probably won't exactly look as you expected.

CIE L*A*B* COLOR SPACE

The problems created by device-dependent color models are obvious: many devices reproduce a given color differently. This issue is made even worse by the fact that color is often converted from one model to another during the design and production processes.

In 1931, the Commission Internationale de l'Eclairage (CIE), an international standards-making body, developed the CIE XYZ color model as the first widely used *device-independent* color space. The model was modified and renamed *CIE L*a*b** in 1976, and is often shortened to simply *L*a*b**.

In the L*a*b* model, color is defined numerically on three axes:

- L* defines the luminance of a color, expressed as a percentage from 0 to 100.
- a* defines the color on the red-green axis, ranging from –128 (green) to +128 (red).
- b* defines the color on the yellow-blue axis, ranging from –128 (blue) to +128 (yellow).

The L*a*b* model describes the physical characteristics of a color without considering any specific output device. This helps to eliminate the confusion created by different gamuts and different reproduction characteristics, and allows us to communicate color based solely on numbers. This color space, though not used for the output of color, is used as an intermediate step for converting from one color model to another. Spectrophotometry, defined earlier in this chapter, measures colors in the L*a*b* color space, so they can then be translated to either the RGB or CMY equivalent.

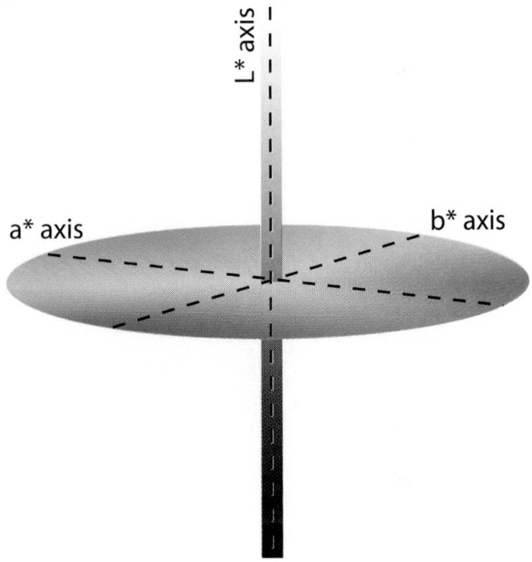

*The L*a*b* color model, showing the L, a, and b axes.*

RGB	Used for designing electronic documents such as Web pages or PDF files that will be distributed electronically.
Web-Safe	Used for designing electronic documents; this is an abbreviated version of RGB, which attempts to ensure the accurate reproduction of color from one monitor to another.
CMYK	Used for designing commercially printed documents.
Hexachrome	Adds green and orange to the CMYK inks to extend the color gamut.
Special Libraries	Used in combination with CMYK to create specific colors outside the CMYK gamut, or as the only colors in a one-, two-, or three-color job.
L*a*b*	Used for converting images from one color space to another; generally not used to define colors in graphics applications.

UNDERSTANDING GAMUT

Different output color models have different ranges or *gamuts* of possible colors. A normal human visual system is capable of distinguishing approximately 16.7 milion different colors. Color reproduction systems, however, are far more limited.

The RGB model, using light as the means to reproduce color, has the largest gamut of the output models. The CMYK gamut is far more limited than the RGB gamut. Many of the brightest and most saturated colors that can be reproduced using light cannot be reproduced using subtractive theory.

The difference in gamut is one of the biggest problems graphic designers face when working with color images. Digital image-capture devices (including scanners and digital cameras) work in RGB space, which, with its larger gamut, can more closely mirror the range of colors in the original scene. Printing, however, requires such images to first be converted or *separated* into the CMYK color space.

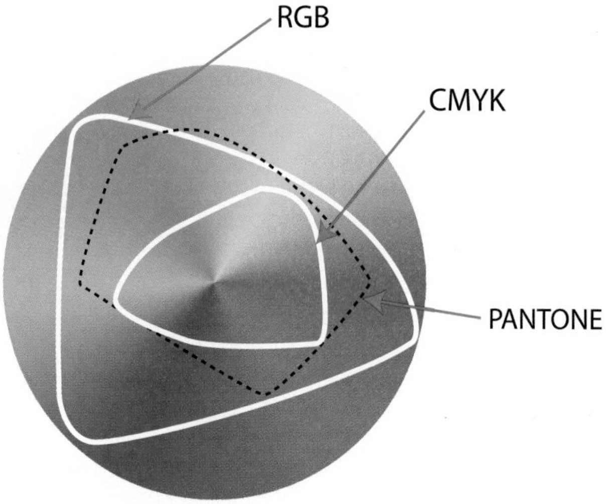

This graphic shows the approximate gamuts of RGB, CMYK, and PANTONE color.

Depending on the images, at least some colors captured with the RGB model likely cannot be reproduced in the more limited gamut of the CMYK color model. These *out-of-gamut* colors pose a challenge to faithfully reproducing the original image. If the conversion from RGB to CMYK is not carefully controlled, *color shift* can result in drastic differences between the original and the printed image. Color management (Chapter 6) and color correction (Chapter 7) are both important tools for quality color reproduction.

A comparison of the RGB (left) and CMYK (right) versions of the same photograph. Notice the differences in the color, especially in the blue umbrella.

Conclusion

There is, of course, far more that could be said about color theory; color science can be extremely complex and confusing to all but the devoted color scientist. In your role as a graphic artist, however, you need to understand the basics of color reproduction to address the issues that affect the colors you use. This chapter has examined the theories that underlie the practical application; we will refer to these concepts frequently throughout the rest of this book. Much time and effort is spent choosing just the right color for a job. A clear understanding of color-reproduction theory can help to ensure that the colors you get in the final output are the ones you chose in the development stage.

CHAPTER 4

Color Images

Images are one of the foundational building blocks of graphic communications. They are used for both print and electronic output; the same image is often repurposed for multiple projects in different media. As a graphic designer, you need to understand the nature of digital-image capture and display to get the best possible results from the images you use.

Before the graphics world went digital, incorporating graphics into design was a complex process, accomplished with traditional media and large graphic-arts cameras or hand-engraved metal printing plates. And of course, Web distribution wasn't even a possibility. As with so many other aspects of technology, incorporating graphics into design has come a long way from manually engraving plates or photographing drawings through screens. Scanning and digital photography make it easy — if not push-button simple — to digitize images. But the ease of using this technology can be misleading. Before they can output images correctly, professional designers first need to understand some basic information about how digital images are created and formatted.

Capturing Colors

The images used in graphic design come from a wide variety of sources, and are captured either by photographing or scanning. Regardless of where images originate, the goal of most designers is usually to accurately reproduce colors as they appear in the original subject. The more steps there are between that original subject and final output, the more chance there is for colors to shift.

Digital cameras produce *first-generation* digital images, those that have only one degree of separation between the original subject and the digital file; any works of art that can be directly scanned are also considered first-generation images. Because there is only a single step separating the original and the digital colors, such images are most likely to capture color accurately. Images such as conventional printed photographs are considered *second-generation* reproductions, because there are two steps between the original and the digital colors — producing the electronic file involves scanning or digitally photographing an image that already reproduces the original. When you use images other than first-generation images in your designs, there are several considerations to ensure that you achieve results that accurately reflect the original image.

WORKING FROM CONVENTIONAL PHOTOGRAPHS

Several technical variables affect the quality of photographs, including film type, speed, and format; emulsion type; and the developing process and paper used (for prints). Each of these factors can cause variation in the color that appears in a final photograph. Add to these factors the lighting conditions and subject matter of a photograph and you can begin to understand why the turquoise waves you saw at Big Sur don't look quite so beautiful when you pick up your pictures from the one-hour developer.

Gamut Shift

When film is developed into photographic prints or transparencies, the colors in the images are reproduced with cyan, magenta, and yellow dyes. The dyes used in photographic reproduction have a large *gamut,* or range of possible colors. The inks used in the printing process — although based on the same cyan, magenta, and yellow primaries — are pigment-based, and have a much smaller gamut than photographic dyes.

When a photograph is reproduced using a mechanical printing process, the range of colors in the photo is compressed into the printable gamut. This inevitably results in *color shift* (a visible change of the color), and can dramatically change the appearance of an image if it is not carefully controlled.

Grain

Photographic film is made up of microscopic grains of light-sensitive material. These grains capture image information, which is eventually processed into a print or transparency. Though not usually apparent in a standard photographic print, grain in a photograph can become pronounced when scanned with a high-resolution scanner. Enlarging an image during scanning further enhances any grain that already exists.

When grain is evident in a scanned image, the grain pattern can destroy fine detail and create a mottled appearance in areas of solid color or subtle tone variation. Slower-rated film typically has the smallest and least evident grain, while faster film can produce significant graininess.

When grain is visible in an image, areas of solid color or subtle tonal variation have a mottled appearance.

Exposure

Different films have varying levels of sensitivity to light. A film's "speed" (also known as the ISO rating) is a measure of the rate at which light is absorbed. Lower numbers (100 or 200) indicate slower light absorption, and higher numbers (1200) indicate faster light absorption.

Slower film is useful for capturing fine detail and subtle tonal variation, such as images of nature. Due to the slow rate of absorption, slower film is most useful in strong daylight conditions. If slower film is used in low or dim light, the images may be underexposed and lack detail unless the camera shutter remains open for a comparatively long period of time.

Faster film is useful for low-light conditions because the available light is absorbed more quickly when the camera shutter opens. High-speed film, however, can result in images that are overexposed if the camera shutter remains open for too long.

Transparencies

Photographic transparencies generally produce sharper scans than photographic prints. Transparencies have a greater tonal range and can retain a greater degree of saturation than prints. Scans from photographic transparencies are typically made from positives, although some scanners are capable of scanning film negatives. Negative transparencies have finer grain and can produce a more accurate tonal range; however, it is difficult to evaluate the content of a negative without first making a color-positive print.

WORKING FROM TRADITIONAL MEDIA

Some graphic-design projects require reproduction of an original work of art that was created with traditional media (such as charcoal, pastels, watercolors, or oil paints). This type of original can be either scanned or photographed, depending on the size and flexibility of the substrate. Three-dimensional sculptures or heavily textured oil paintings, for example, must be photographed; flat works, such as watercolors, can be scanned if they fit on the scanner bed or around the scanner drum.

The main challenge when reproducing original works of art is that each medium has a different color gamut, and each gamut is considerably different than the gamut of printing inks. Digitally capturing the original art introduces one degree of color shift because the colors are compressed into the dynamic range of the capturing device. The colors are further compressed when the image is converted to CMYK for commercial printing. Careful calibration and color-management techniques (discussed in Chapter 6) must be used throughout the process to maintain the appearance and integrity of the original.

WORKING FROM PREVIOUSLY PRINTED WORK

Any images that have been previously printed on a commercial press are at least *third-generation* — incorporating them into graphic-design layouts involves scanning something that has already been photographed or scanned, then printed. If you have absolutely no choice but to scan an image that has already been printed, you must first accept that you will be working with (at least) a third-generation reproduction of the image, and that the quality of the final image will not be ideal. When an image is printed, it is created using a pattern of halftone dots in varying sizes that create the illusion of continuous tone. Though the human eye cannot generally perceive the dot pattern, high-resolution scanners can.

Scanning a previously printed image almost always results in a scanned picture of dots. This can be partially corrected by using a series of filters to *descreen* the image during scanning, or by alternately blurring and sharpening the image once it is scanned. The problem with these techniques is that descreening and blurring filters decrease an image's sharpness, compromising detail and quality for the sake of reproducing a previously printed image.

COMPARING IMAGE-CAPTURE TECHNOLOGIES

There are many different types of scanners available, from the low-end $59 desktop flatbed scanner to the high-end $150,000 commercial drum scanner. In between these two extremes, there are many options. Some scanners are used only to scan reflective copy; others scan transparencies; still others are limited to scanning 35-mm film. Some scan large originals; others are capable of scanning letter-sized pages, but produce the best results only in the middle of the scanner bed.

The original EPS file.

The scanned file with no descreening.

The image scanned using the scanner's built-in descreening algorithm.

The scanned image descreened using a series of Gaussian blur and unsharp masking filters in Adobe Photoshop.

Scanning previously printed images results in the visibility of the dot pattern used to print the image, unless some blurring or descreening is used.

There are two basic types of scanners in use today. The traditional print-shop drum scanner is based on a *photomultiplier tube* (PMT) — a very accurate sensor. The photographic original is attached to a clear plastic drum and rotated past a group of PMT sensors — usually one each for red, green, and blue (RGB) input, and a fourth that handles the task of sharpening the digital image (a process called "unsharp masking").

The smaller and less expensive flatbed scanner uses a *charge-coupled device* (CCD) sensor. An array of three CCD sensors collects the three channels of red, green, and blue data. CCDs are much smaller than PMTs, which makes CCD technology more viable for small capture devices such as digital cameras, desktop scanners, and digital video cameras.

Digital cameras also use CCD technology, based on a honeycomb of sensing cells called "pixels." Commercial-quality megapixel digital cameras can capture over a million pixels per image; current models ship with 3–5 megapixels, and high-megapixel models have recently started to appear on the market.

Only a few years ago, if you wanted an image with sufficient quality for commercial printing, you had to find a trade shop with a drum scanner. But image-capture technology, like everything else, has evolved rapidly — digital cameras and some flatbed scanners can now produce sufficient quality for most applications.

Many traditional photographers argue that the color range (called the "dynamic range") of a digital camera is more limited than a traditional scan of a transparency film image; in addition, there's no original from which to rescan if a serious problem arises. These drawbacks are countered by a digital camera's ability to remove several steps from the process, which eases the pressure of today's shorter production cycles.

Traditional drum scanners are very expensive. When compared to the newest generation of flatbed scanners, many designers and service providers have decided that the less expensive flatbed scanners are sufficient for their requirements. This does not mean that professional magazine covers are scanned with a $45 scanner purchased at a local office-supply store. There is a huge difference between the capture capabilities of consumer-level and professional-level flatbed scanners. High-end professional flatbed scanners usually cost $1,000 or more. When buying a scanner, you usually get what you pay for.

Expensive, professional-quality scanners and cameras typically offer precise control over the capturing capability of each color filter. An expensive scanner with lots of buttons and knobs, however, does not guarantee a quality scan. The range of settings provides far greater control, but also allows for many more problems — including color cast — if the controls are not set correctly.

> The many different types of scanners and digital cameras can capture varying ranges of colors. Inexpensive, consumer-level cameras and scanners frequently have predefined plug-and-play-type capture settings for "Nature," "People," and other common subject content. These settings adjust the internal device filters, for example, paying more attention to green shades in Nature. This type of setting almost always produces some degree of color cast that must be corrected later.

There are many professional services that, for a fee, scan images on high-quality scanners that are carefully calibrated and adjusted to produce high-quality images that require little or no color correction. If you choose to do your own scanning, you should take the time to learn proper scanning techniques to minimize the amount of correction you need to do later in the production cycle.

Optical and Interpolated Resolution

A scanner's resolution is determined by the optical resolution of the capture technology and the step speed of the motor. Scanner resolution is usually specified with two numbers, such as 1200 × 2400 dpi. The first number is the number of dots (or, more appropriately, samples) that the scanner optics can sample. The second number is the number of steps the scanner's motor can make in a single inch down the length of the scanner bed. In other words, a 1200 × 2400-dpi scanner has a 1200-dpi CCD and a motor that goes slow enough to scan 2400 lines per inch as it moves down the bed. These numbers, called the scanner's "optical resolution," are the most important specification for any scanner.

> When scanners are sold, their resolution is described in "dots per inch" (dpi). A more accurate term, however, would be "pixels per inch" (ppi), which is the measurement used to describe the resolution of the images that are created from scans. To be most accurate, we should use the term "samples per inch" (spi) to refer to the scanner's imaging capabilities.

It's fairly common, however, to see marketing materials for a 1200 × 2400-dpi scanner promise "Up to 9600 dpi!" So what does this mean? Any resolution higher than the scanner's optical resolution will be *interpolated*, or artificially generated by hardware or software. A chip inside the scanner uses an algorithm to create new data by averaging adjacent dots, essentially filling in the spaces to create, for example, 2400 dpi when the scanning CCD is only rated to capture half that number.

Interpolated resolution creates pixels of averaged color and intensity between every real pixel. For example, a new pixel between adjacent pixels with green values of 50 and 60 will have a green value of 55 — the transition would be 50, 55, 60. (The red and blue channels would also be interpolated accordingly.) Interpolation can artificially increase the resolution — and thus, the physical size — of the resulting image, but it does not add detail or improve quality. The image will have more data, and the file will be physically larger than the original; despite the higher resolution, however, any fine detail will be compromised, and the image will have an overall blurry look.

Color Depth

A scanner's *color depth* (also called "bit depth") defines the number of colors that can be captured for each pixel. The concept of color depth refers to the science underlying computer displays and video cards. The number of available colors is based on how much memory is available for each pixel. Every bit of computer data has two possible values: off or on. When applied to color, this translates to the color depth required to display different types of color.

- 1-bit color has only two possible values for each pixel — black (off or 0) or white (on or 1). High-resolution line art is often saved as 1-bit because these files have only two colors — black and white.
- 8-bit color can contain one of 256 (2^8) numeric values (ranging from 0 to 255) for each pixel. Grayscale and monotone images can be safely displayed in 8-bit color.
- 24-bit color uses 8 bits for each color channel (red, green, and blue) for each pixel. In other words, each color channel can have a value from 0–255, resulting in 16.7 million possible colors ($[2^8]^3$ or 256 × 256 × 256). RGB images require 24-bit color to accurately reproduce the range of colors in an original image.

> A monitor's color depth depends on the computer's video card, which determines the memory available to display colors. Regardless of how many colors your images contain, you should always remember that they will often be viewed on computers with older video cards, with a smaller color depth.

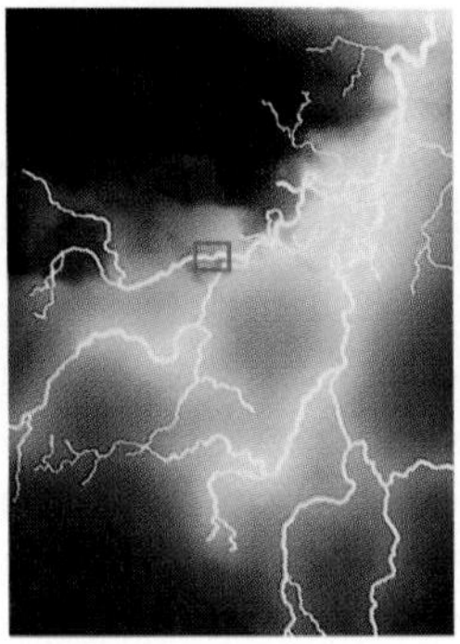

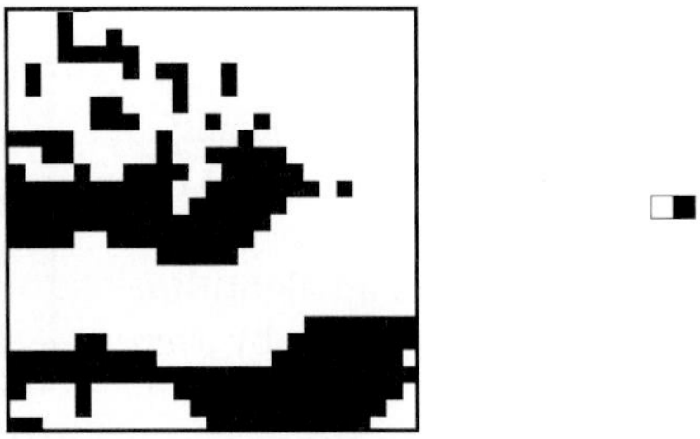

1-Bit Color

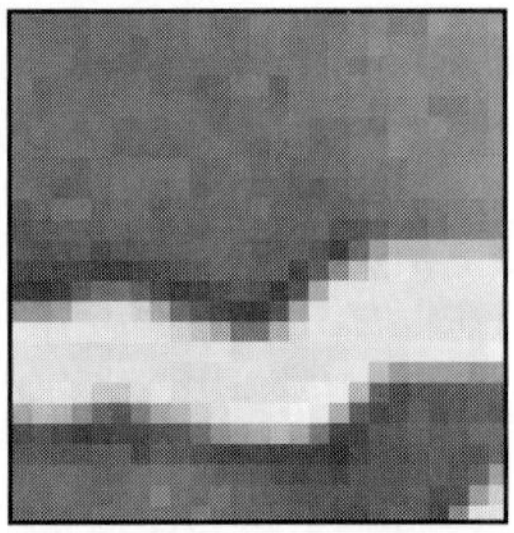

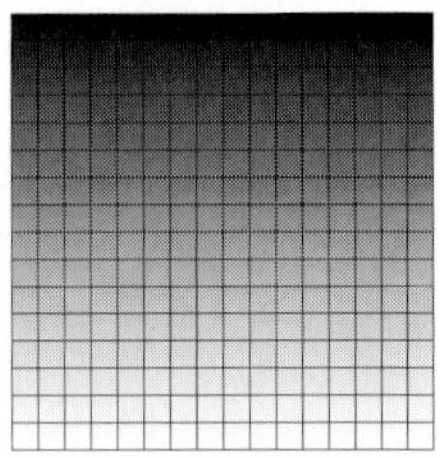

8-Bit Color

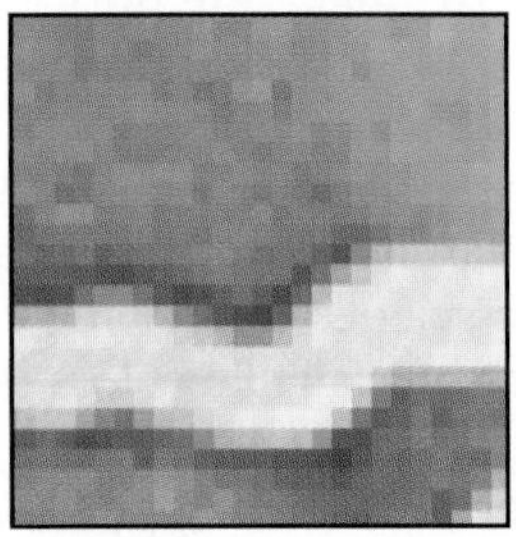

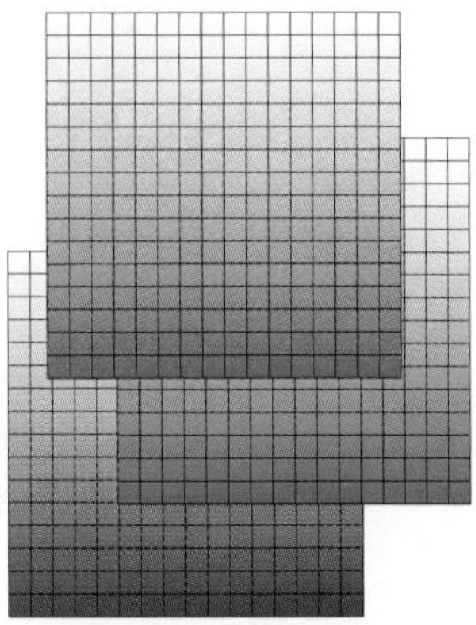

24-Bit Color

Density and Dynamic Range

So if 24-bit color can reproduce the 16.7 million colors discernible to the human eye, why do some scanners offer 30, 36, or more bits? To answer that question, we need to first define *image density*, which is a measure of an image's brightness, ranging from 0 (white) to 4 (black). Scanners and digital cameras are typically rated with minimum and maximum density capabilities ("Dmin" and "Dmax," respectively). The *dynamic range* is the difference between the Dmin and Dmax values.

Dmax = 3.2 Dmin = 0.1

Range = Dmax – Dmin = 3.2 – 0.1 = 3.1

- Photographic prints usually have a dynamic range less than 2.0.
- Color negatives typically have a dynamic range around 2.8.
- Slide film generally has a dynamic range higher than 3.0.

Higher density means that less light is transmitted through film or reflected from paper. When an image is scanned, the scanner's CCD measures the intensity of light transmitted or reflected, and calculates the appropriate RGB values. Most 24-bit scanners have a relatively low Dmax and dynamic range, which means that details in the darkest areas of scans can be lost.

Increasing the number of bits increases the number of shades that can be captured for each individual pixel. A 30- or 36-bit scanner allows greater distinction between very small variations in color, which means that greater detail can be captured in scans. Greater bit depth is necessary to capture the entire dynamic range of color negatives and slide film. Practically applied, greater bit depth increases the dynamic range. Greater dynamic range can capture more detail in dark shadow areas when scanning positive images and in highlights when scanning negatives.

Types of Images

In graphic design, you will work with two primary types of pictures — vector graphics and raster images. (Line art, a third "category" of images, is actually a specific type of raster image, with unique requirements and characteristics.) Each type of picture has specific benefits and drawbacks, depending on your intended outcome.

VECTOR GRAPHICS

Most digital graphics — including illustrations, page-layout elements, and fonts — can be described as a series of *vectors,* which are mathematical descriptors of lines and geometric shapes. This type of graphic is *resolution independent*; it can be freely scaled and adopts its resolution at the time of printing from the capabilities of the output device. One of the advantages of vector art is its feature of unlimited scaling. Vector graphics adopt the highest possible resolution of the intended output device, so you can freely scale, resize, rotate, or otherwise manipulate them without worrying about degrading the illustration quality.

RASTER IMAGES

A raster image is a group of individual *rasters* (bits or pixels) arranged in a grid of rows and columns (called a "bitmap"). In contrast to vector files, which are resolution independent, raster files are *resolution dependent* — their resolution is determined at the time of *input* (scanning or capture with a digital camera). Each pixel is a tiny square of color, and thousands of pixels next to each other in different colors and shades create the illusion of smooth, continuous-tone shading when the image is printed.

When we discuss the resolution of a raster image, we use the term "pixels per inch" or simply "ppi." This measure refers to the number of pixels (short for "picture elements") that exist in one horizontal or vertical inch of a digital raster file. The resolution of a raster file specifies the number of pixels within it. A 3 × 5-in. one-color file created at

The same file is reproduced as both a raster image (top) and a vector graphic (bottom). The right images show the results of enlarging each type of file to 1600%.

72 ppi, for example, contains 216 pixels in every row and 360 pixels in every column; simple multiplication reveals that the image contains a total of 77,760 pixels.

Because raster images have an absolute resolution, their output quality depends directly upon the size at which the image is printed. If a 3 × 5-in. raster graphic created at 72 ppi is resized to 200% (6 × 10 in.), there will still be only 77,760 pixels available to fill the extra space; the resizing reduces the resolution of the image to 36 ppi and makes the image appear much coarser or *pixelated* when it is printed.

LINE ART

Line art is a special type of raster image made up entirely of 100% solid areas. Each pixel in a line-art image has only two options: black or white. Examples of line art are UPC bar codes and pen drawings.

A bitmap or line-art image has only two colors — black and white. There are no shades of gray or colors.

To reproduce line art, you should scan the image at the highest resolution that the output device is capable of using. For example, a 600-dpi (dots per inch) printer can create a maximum of 600 × 600 (360,000) dots in one square inch; you should give the printer as much information as it can use, which in this case would be 600 pixels per inch. If the art were created and printed only at 300 ppi, then the printer would have to skip to every other possible space to put a dot. The result is known as "stair-stepping" or "bitmapping."

Most modern laser printers image at 600 to 1200 dpi, but film on an imagesetter is typically produced at a much higher resolution, usually at least 2540 dpi. Fortunately, the human eye is not sensitive enough to discern bitmapping beyond 1200 dpi. Thus, the best rule for scanning line art for commercial printing is to always use 1200 dpi.

Line art refers to high-contrast, monochrome illustrations or artwork. In common desktop-computer jargon, the term "line art" is sometimes used to describe vector-based illustrations such as those created in Illustrator or FreeHand. Be aware of this distinction. By its traditional definition, a line-art file might be rendered as a vector-based image or a bitmap, raster image.

Working with Resolution

Once an image is digitized, you can easily resize it in an image-editing application or scale it in a print or Web-page layout. Resizing an image is simply a matter of taking an existing file and changing its physical dimensions — for example, enlarging a 4.5 × 6-in. image to 9 × 12 in. so the image will cover an entire letter-size page. You can permanently change the image information using an image-editing application such as Photoshop, or you can scale the image to 200% in a layout application. There are, however, several problems with both techniques.

Remember that every raster image has a defined, specific resolution that is established when the image is created. If you scanned an image to be 3 inches high by 5 inches wide at 150 ppi, that image has 450 pixels in each vertical column and 750 pixels in each horizontal row. Simply resizing the

The original image (right) was scanned to be 1.75 × 1.4 in. at 300 ppi, resulting in 525 pixels in each row. When the file is enlarged 300% (below), those 525 pixels must extend across 5.25 inches instead of 1.75. The resolution drops to 100 ppi, resulting in a severe loss of quality.

image stretches or compresses those pixels into a different physical space, but does not add or remove pixel information. If you resize the 3 × 5-image to 6 × 10 in. (200% of the original), the 450 pixels in each column will be forced to extend across 6 inches instead of 3, causing a marked loss of quality.

The *effective resolution* of an image is the resolution calculated after any scaling is taken into account. This number is equally — and sometimes more — important than the original image resolution. The effective resolution can be calculated with a fairly simple equation:

Original resolution ÷ (% magnification ÷ 100) = Effective resolution

If a 300-ppi image is magnified 150%, the effective resolution is:

300 ppi ÷ 1.5 = 200 ppi

In other words, the more you enlarge a raster image, the lower its effective resolution becomes. In general, you can make an image 10% or 15% larger without significant adverse effects; the more you enlarge an image, the worse the results. Even Photoshop, which offers very sophisticated formulas (called "algorithms") for sizing images, cannot guarantee perfect results.

DOWNSIZING

You can take advantage of effective resolution if you want to print a low-resolution image created at a large enough physical size. Consumer-level digital cameras work on this principle. The camera captures all images at a set resolution (usually 72 ppi). The different quality settings (high, medium, and low, or some similar variations) do not change the capturing resolution. Instead, they affect the physical size of the resulting image; "high" quality settings produce very large pictures while "low" settings produce small pictures.

When you first open a "high"-quality picture in an image-editing application, you might have a picture that is 28 inches wide at 72 ppi. If you resize the image to 25%, or 7 inches wide, you will increase the effective resolution to 288 ppi — enough for most printing applications.

RESAMPLING

In general, you should always scan your images to be the size you will use in your final job. If you absolutely must resize a digital image, you can use a technique called *resampling* to achieve better results than simply changing the image size. Image-editing software uses mathematical formulas either to generate extra pixel data (when you're increasing the image size), or to determine which pixels to discard (when you're reducing the image size).

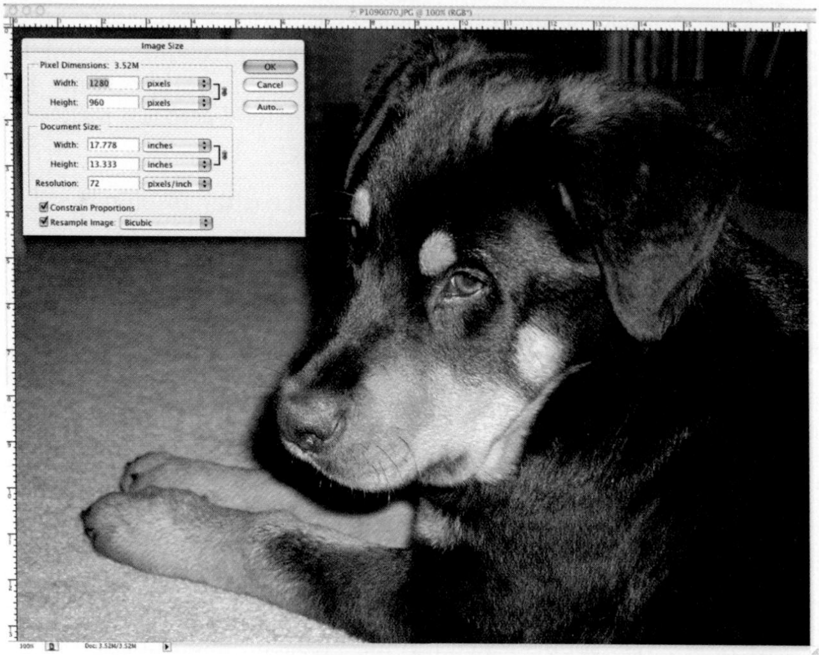

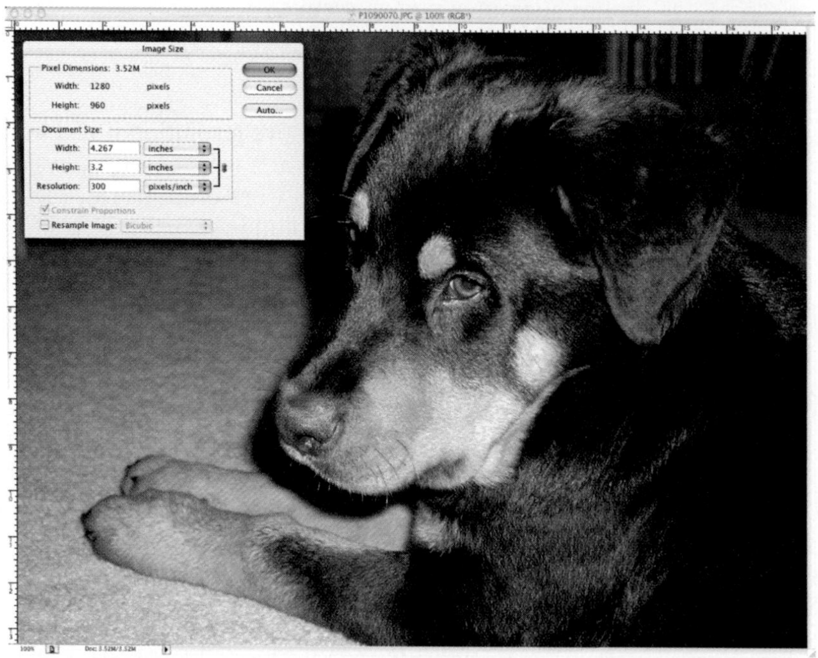

The original image (above) is 72 ppi, with physical dimensions of 17.778 × 13.333 in., translating to 1280 pixels horizontally and 960 pixels vertically. When the image is resized (below), the same number of pixels is compressed into a smaller physical space so the resulting image has 300 pixels per inch. Both images have the same number of pixels.

There are three different interpolation methods available for resampling. Each offers a tradeoff between quality and speed:

- **Bicubic Resampling.** This method creates the most accurate pixel information for continuous-tone images; it also takes the longest to process, and produces a softer image. To understand how this option works, think of a square bisected both horizontally and vertically — bicubic resampling averages the value of all four of those squares (pixels) to interpolate the new information.

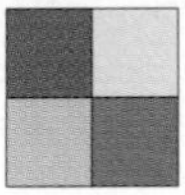

- **Bilinear Resampling.** This is a medium-quality resampling method. Returning to the square example, bilinear resampling averages two of the four squares to create new information. Bilinear resampling is faster than bicubic, and retains better contrast.
- **Nearest Neighbor.** This is a low-quality but quick resampling method. Nearest neighbor interpolates new pixel information based on only one of the squares in the grid, usually resulting in an image with a blocky appearance.

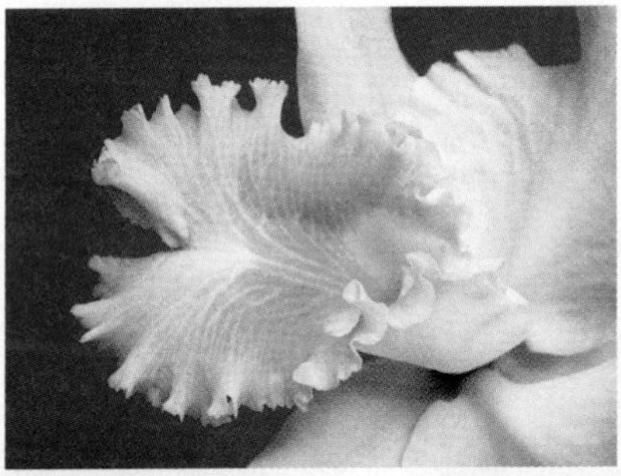

The original image (left) was resampled using the different methods:

bicubic resampling (bottom left), bilinear resampling (bottom middle), and nearest neighbor (bottom right).

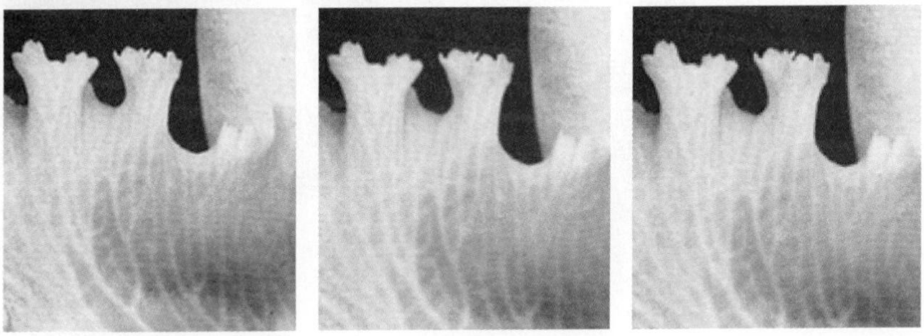

THROWING AWAY PIXELS

Higher resolution means larger file sizes, which translates to longer processing time for printing or longer download time for the Internet. When you scale an image to a smaller size, simply resizing can produce files with far greater effective resolution than you need. Resampling allows you to reduce the physical size of an image without increasing the resolution, resulting in a smaller file size.

The caveat here is that once you throw away pixels, they are gone. If you later try to re-enlarge the smaller image, you will not achieve the same quality as the original (before it was reduced). You should always save reduced images as copies instead of overwriting the original.

The original image (top) was scanned at 300 ppi with a physical size of 5 × 3.75 in. The image was then resized to a smaller 3 × 2.25 in. to fit in a catalog. If you delete or overwrite the original file, then later need the image to be 5 × 3.75 again, your only chance is to resample the reduced image. The bottom image shows the result of bicubic resampling back to the original size. The quality is passable, but some of the fine detail is lost.

Image File Formats

When you save graphics and images, you have to choose from a large number of file formats. Each option has advantages and disadvantages, depending on what you want to accomplish with the file. Different types of image content, color, and intended output media dictate the file format that is appropriate in any given situation.

FORMATS FOR PRINT

There are two primary formats for printing images, and dozens of others less frequently encountered. Most desktop-publishing applications allow you to save your files in a variety of file formats. In the real world though, there are only two file formats you should ever use for printing — EPS and TIFF. Straying from these established standards will inevitably cause problems with your files.

> Though most other formats (including GIF, WMF, BMP, PICT, and JPEG) work just fine when printing composites to a desktop laser printer, they lack the information necessary for a high-end RIP to properly image film. The RIP may fail to print the image or completely crash. Colors will either not print at all, or incorrect color separations will result in the same information appearing on every printing plate.

Tagged Image File Format (TIFF)

TIFF is a format used *only* for raster (bitmapped) images, usually generated by scanning analog art or photos. If you draw a vector line in a graphic, it cannot be saved into the TIFF format unless it is *rasterized* or *parsed* into a grid of pixels. TIFF files can be one-color (monochrome), grayscale, or continuous-tone color.

Most grayscale and CMYK images can be saved safely in this format. If you use duotones or clipping paths, you should save the file as EPS.

Encapsulated PostScript (EPS)

EPS is the format used widely for vector-art graphics. It handles files containing text, shapes, and lines. Because EPS files can also handle raster-image graphics, you need to examine each file to determine whether it holds vector graphics, raster graphics, or a combination of both. An EPS file name has the .eps suffix.

This file format uses an adaptation of the PostScript page-description language to produce

> All vector graphics need to be saved as Encapsulated PostScript files (EPS), but not all EPS files are vector graphics. Don't make the mistake of assuming that just because a file carries the .eps extension that it has the properties of vector graphics. Most images can be saved in EPS format.

a "placeable" image file. All vector art should be saved in this format, as well as images with clipping paths, and duotone images. When you save a file as EPS, make certain that you use the TIFF preview option instead of the Macintosh-specific PICT preview.

Desktop Color Separation (DCS) Files

Desktop Color Separation (DCS) is an extension of the EPS format; it is a pre-separated format that includes a color preview for placement into the page layout and the external cyan, magenta, yellow, and black components needed for final output on a commercial press (described in Chapter 5). When you save an image as DCS1, you create five file components.

As you design the layout, you can place the EPS preview file into the document page. When a page containing a DCS image is output, the RIP (raster-image processor) calls the appropriate color-separation files to replace the low-resolution placement image.

If an image includes spot colors, the additional channels appear in their own files when you save as DCS:

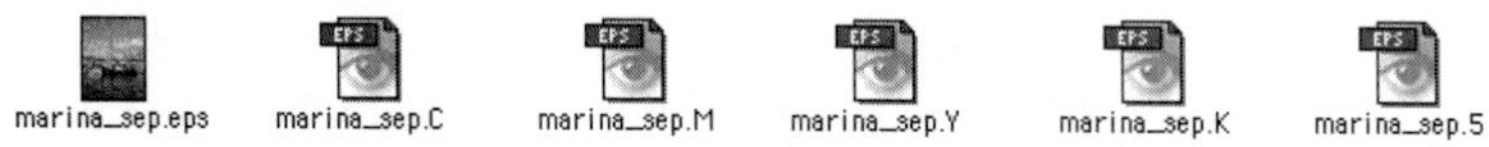

The DCS format proved to be a customer-service nightmare for many service bureaus. Managing five files for each image proved to be difficult at best, and many customers couldn't understand why they could not modify the preview image. DCS 2.0, introduced in 2000, extended the capabilities of the original DCS format. The DCS2 format includes all the separation information in one file, with individual tables for each color channel. You can save plate separations for multiple spot colors as well as CMYK, which is especially useful if you are using the Hexachrome system. Photoshop images in Multichannel mode, or in CMYK mode using spot channels, must be saved as DCS2 before you can import them into page layouts.

> The DCS format allows an output provider the option of doing high-quality scans and then sending the low-resolution file back to the customer to be used to construct the page layout. The low-resolution preview works well for on-screen layout and proofs; the high-resolution separations are re-linked when the finished layout is ready for output.

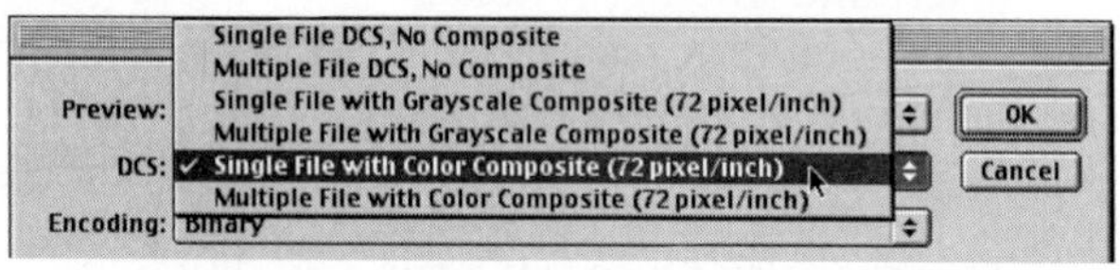

Saving a file using the DCS2 format gives you the option to save the file as a composite or with separate files for each color channel.

FORMATS FOR THE WEB

When saving files for Web distribution, the format you use will affect the display of the colors in the exported file. Although JPEG and GIF files are not suitable for commercial printing, they are the standard formats for Web development.

JPEG

JPEG is the format of choice for continuous-tone images, such as scanned images and photos from a digital camera. The JPEG format compresses image information using a *lossy* compression algorithm, which means information is lost in the resulting file. Most software allows you to choose from predefined-but-vague compression levels (Low, Medium, High, or Maximum), or you can choose a specific quality percentage. These choices refer to the quality of the resulting image, not the amount of compression applied. Remember that the higher quality you want, the less compression should be applied.

The JPEG file format can store 24-bit color, making it an excellent choice for photographs. It is not well suited for text or graphics, since its block-by-block compression algorithm introduces a blurring effect to the images. Within each block, differences in brightness are retained, but subtle color changes are lost. Despite this loss of color information, the image quality is acceptable, even at maximum compression.

"Low" JPEG compression

"Medium" JPEG compression

"High" JPEG compression

"Maximum" JPEG compression

GIF

GIF is an 8-bit file format typically used for vector graphics or rasterized artwork. It is ideally suited for files with large areas of solid color, but does not do well with continuous-tone images that have subtle color variations.

When you save a file in the GIF format, all the colors are mapped to a color table called "indexed color." Indexed color is an 8-bit color model in which the specific 256 values are based on the colors in the image. Graphics software allows you to specify the method used to remap colors, typically from four options:

- **Perceptual.** This gives priority to colors to which the human eye is more sensitive.

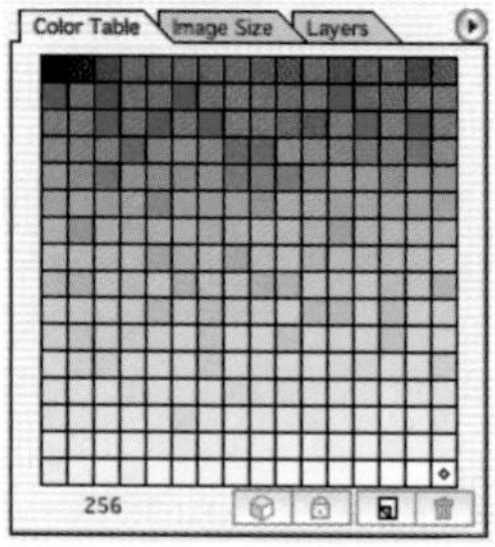

- **Selective.** This is similar to Perceptual, but favors broad areas of color. This option usually produces the best results.

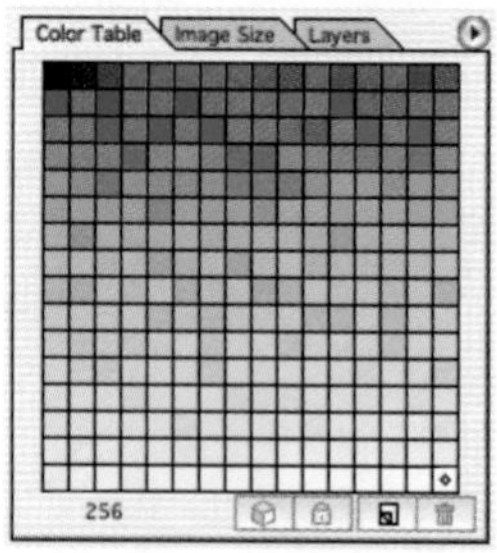

- **Adaptive.** This samples colors appearing most commonly in the image. For example, an image with only the colors green and blue produces a color table made primarily of greens and blues. Most images concentrate colors in particular areas of the spectrum.

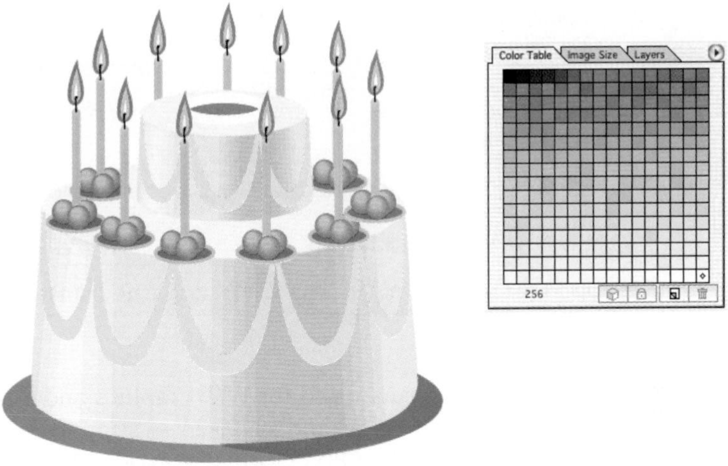

- **Web.** This uses the standard 216-color Web-safe color table. This option creates larger files, and can result in drastic color shift.

Because indexed color can only support 256 possible shades, there is obviously a limit to the subtle differences you can include in an image using this format. To create the illusion of more possible colors, the GIF format supports *dithering*. This technique is similar to the process used in color printing (see Chapter 5) in which colors are rendered as overlapping dots to create the illusion of additional colors without increasing the number of colors actually saved in the file. Dithering should be used with care, because it can destroy fine lines and detail.

The same image is reproduced with (left) and without (right) dithering.

BMP	Bitmapped, Windows raster format.
WMF	Windows MetaFile.
PICT	Mac PICTure format. Based on QuickDraw.
JPEG	Joint Photographic Experts Group. Cross-platform lossy compression format; used for Web images.
GIF	Graphics Interchange Format. Limited to 256 colors; used for Web graphics.
PNG	Portable Network Graphics. Can support 8- or 24-bit color; raster or vector format for Web graphics.
TIFF	Tagged Image File Format. Cross-platform raster format for print images.
EPS	Encapsulated PostScript. Vector or raster format for print graphics and images.
DCS	Desktop Color Separation. Used for CMYK (separated) images in print workflow.

PNG

PNG is a third format used for Web graphics and images. Two versions of the format — PNG-8 and PNG-24 — support 8-bit and 24-bit color respectively. The PNG format's broad color gamut provides the best way to display photographic images for which subtle shades are critical to the quality of the image. Like GIF, PNG files support dithering to improve the appearance of colors in 8-bit files.

Preparing Images for the Web

Since the advent of the Internet, many designers have worked on documents destined for electronic publication and distribution. There are some special considerations associated with reproducing color for electronic media. When designing for the Web, you need to recognize that users have different computer systems, and they can customize several important settings of those systems. Many factors — including operating system, video card, brand of monitor, and monitor resolution — can affect the way color is displayed for any particular Internet user.

USER-ADJUSTABLE SETTINGS

Many industry experts claim that advances in technology have eliminated most of the variation in color from one system to the next. In theory, this is true; if everyone on earth were using the very latest in color-management and video-display technology, you could safely assume most people will see the same color you do.

> This discussion refers to the practical use of monitor resolution, not the physical dot matrix of the monitor. The monitor's dot pitch is a specific number that cannot be changed.

There are a number of variables involved that make it very difficult — if not impossible — to guarantee that the colors in your designs will appear the

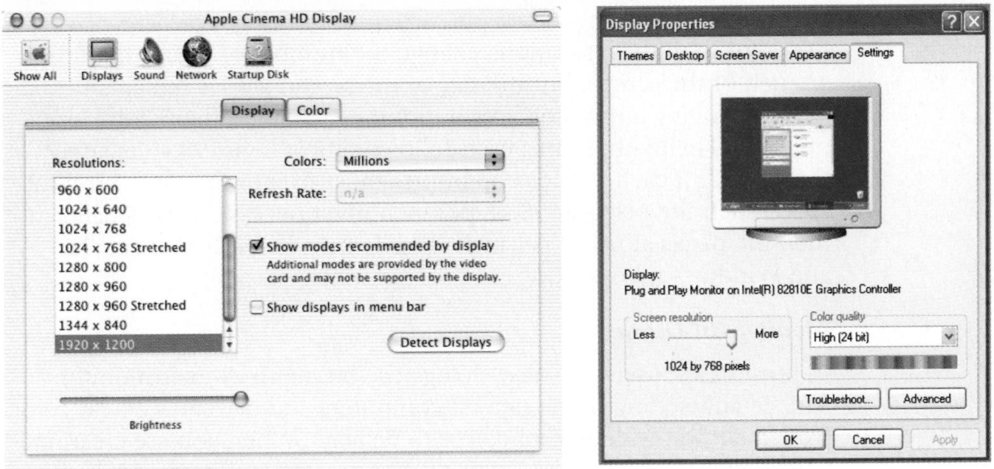

Depending on the type of computer you use, display settings are accessed in the System Preferences or Control Panels.

same to every user. Because it is very easy for users to adjust the resolution and bit-depth settings of their monitors, it makes sense for designers to understand how those settings can affect the display of electronic images.

Monitor Resolution

Many people share the common belief that an Apple monitor displays 72 pixels per inch and a Windows monitor displays 96 pixels per inch. Although in some cases this might be true, it is a misleading belief. Virtually every computer system allows the user to change the monitor's resolution.

Changing the monitor's resolution can have a major effect on the size at which the images in your documents display. For example, a 23-in. Apple Cinema HD Display monitor has a horizontal viewing space of about 19.5 inches. The recommended resolution for this monitor, as shown in the Display Preferences window, is 1920 × 1200 ppi. The first number (1920) shows the number of pixels displayed horizontally across the monitor.

$$1920 \text{ pixels} \div 19.5 \text{ inches} = 98.46 \text{ pixels per inch}$$

Thus, the default (preferred) setting for this monitor is 98.46 ppi. At this setting, text and graphics appear quite small. Many people, of course, prefer text and graphics to appear larger, so they set the resolution lower than 1920 × 1200. (People with poor eyesight sometimes set monitor resolution to the equivalent of a large-print book.) At the next lowest setting for the Apple Cinema Display, the monitor resolution is 1344 × 840 ppi; the monitor is still 19.5 inches wide.

$$1344 \text{ pixels} \div 19.5 \text{ inches} = 68.92 \text{ pixels per inch}$$

At a resolution of only 68.92 ppi, text and images appear larger. Different monitor resolutions change the number of pixels that fit in an inch of the screen, but the size of the screen always remains the same; changing a monitor's resolution only changes the relative size of pixels. The math, in this case, follows simple logic: 98.46 is larger than 68.92. If each of those quantities must fit into the same physical space, then the pixels at 98.46 per inch must necessarily be smaller than the pixels at 68.92 per inch. This is true for both Macintosh and Windows monitors.

Monitor Bit Depth

In most cases, users can also change the bit depth of their monitors. The default setting of the newest computers and drivers is 24-bit color (which allows "Millions" of colors to display). When you are creating your designs, you can choose instead to display 16-bit color (which will allow only "Thousands" of colors to display) — doing this will give you a better idea of how colors will appear on older or less-expensive monitors.

A computer's video memory limits the color depth that can be displayed at a specific resolution. Remember that "24-bit" is, technically, a designation of the amount of memory required to display full RGB color. For each pixel, each color channel requires 8 bits or 1 byte (there are 8 bits in a byte) of memory; thus, each pixel requires 3 bytes of memory to be able to display images using millions of colors.

To determine the video memory required to display millions of colors, first determine the number of pixels at a given resolution, for example:

1024 x 768 = 786,432 pixels

Then multiply the number of pixels by 3 bytes:

786,432 pixels x 3 bytes per pixel = 2,359,296 bytes or 2.4 megabytes

Higher-resolution settings require more memory, and lower-resolution settings require less memory. In most cases, the computer controls are sophisticated enough to present only possible options. Your resolution settings will be limited based on the number of colors you want to see; resolutions that require too much memory will be grayed out or unavailable.

ADJUSTING IMAGES

Because you can't predict the resolution of every user's monitor, it is difficult to know how to size images for Web distribution. The standard for Web images has long been 72 ppi or 96 ppi. As you just learned, however, the resolution of every monitor can be different — so how do you determine the most appropriate resolution and size for the images in your designs?

Resizing vs. Resampling

When displayed on screen, the display resolution determines how an image's pixels will be displayed. We scanned the following image at 150 ppi, then opened it in Internet Explorer. The title bar displays the file name and the image size in pixels; the image's resolution isn't mentioned anywhere.

We resized the same image to 25 pixels per inch without resampling (changing the number of pixels). The browser's title bar shows the same number of total pixels, and the image appears exactly the same as the one with 150 ppi. The point is, the appearance of an image depends on *the number of pixels* in the image, not the pixels per inch defined in the image.

To change the size at which an image displays on the Web, you have to change the number of pixels in the image by resampling. By resampling the same image to 72 ppi (instead of simply resizing it), the number of pixels is reduced and the image takes up much less space on the screen.

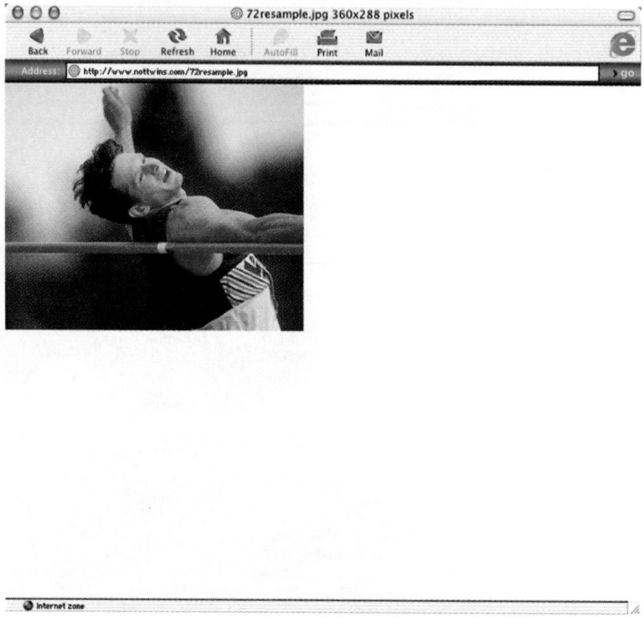

Of course, most Web-design software allows you to scale images, or define specific sizes for images within a page layout. Without this type of control over the appearance of our work, there wouldn't be much "design" in Web design. Web-layout software essentially allows you to override the monitor settings by defining the amount of space an image should take. The concept of effective resolution, however, applies to Web images just as it does to print images.

If you enlarge an image in a layout application, you only stretch out the existing pixels. Rather than displaying at the monitor's optimum setting, you can specify, for example, that a 360 × 324-pixel image should exist in a 10 × 9-in. space. The image that appears will only have 36 pixels per inch — creating a poor-quality, bitmapped effect.

Reducing an image in a layout can result in more effective resolution than you need. If you scale an image to 50% in a layout application, you end up with (roughly) twice the number of pixels necessary to display the image. Removing the unnecessary pixels through resampling reduces file size and download time without sacrificing much quality.

Web-Safe Colors

Remember, you should always consider the output medium when you are designing with color. Obviously, you have no way of knowing exactly what resolution and color settings different users have applied to their computer systems. When designing for the Internet, you have to make educated guesses and use colors that will *likely* be viewable by *most* users (the least common denominator).

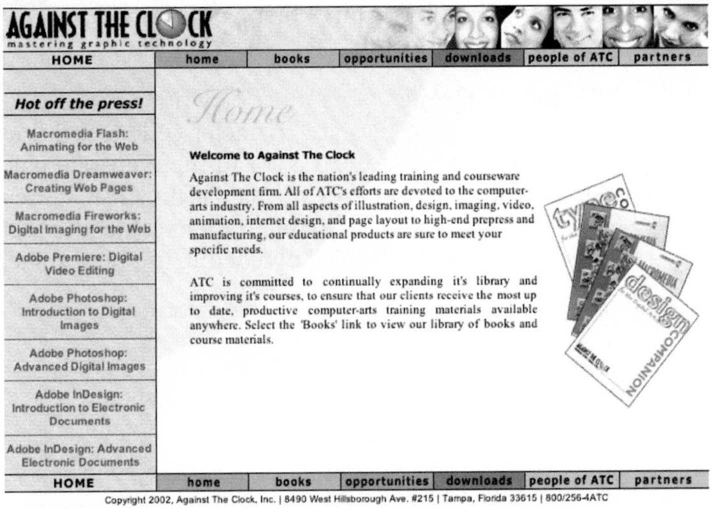

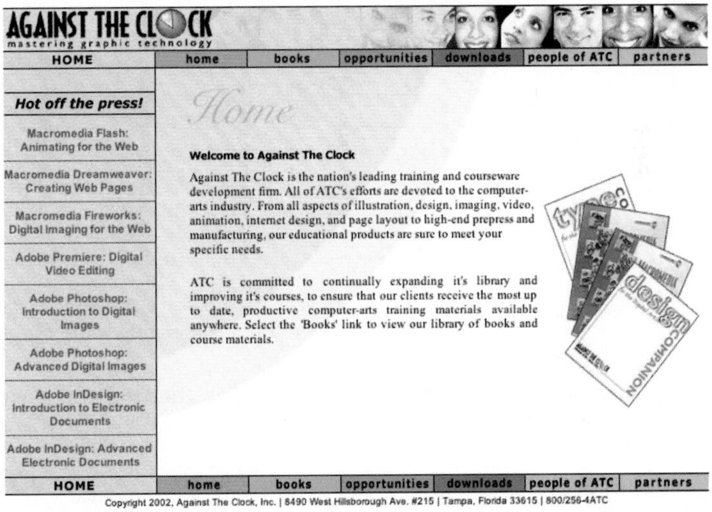

The Against The Clock Web site displayed in thousands of colors (top) and millions of colors (bottom). Notice the difference in color, especially in the background of the main area.

To be certain that most people will see the same colors in your work, you should — whenever possible — use "Web-safe" color in your designs. Web-safe colors are drawn from a palette limited to the 216 colors that can be faithfully reproduced even on 8-bit monitors. Most illustration, image-editing, and Web-design applications include a palette or library of Web-safe colors from which you can select colors for your work.

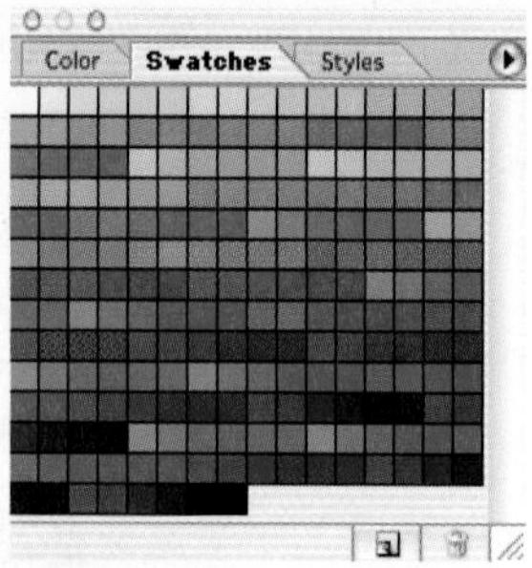

Because Web-safe colors must be written into HTML code, each of them is identified by a six-character code called the "hexadecimal value" of that color. Each color in the Web-safe palette has a unique hexadecimal value, in the format "#RRGGBB." After the number sign, the first two characters define the red value, the second two define the green value, and the third two define the blue value.

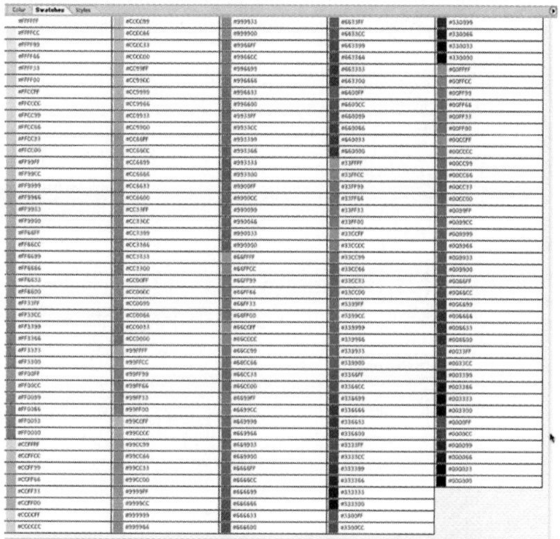

Photoshop's Web-safe palette shown in List mode, where you can see the hexadecimal value for each color.

In the Web-safe palette, each color channel can have one of six possible values:

00	33	66	99	CC	FF

If you remember basic math skills, you can easily compute that six to the power of three (6^3) equals 216 possible color values. In other words, every possible combination of these values results in the 216 colors that can safely be displayed in 8-bit color mode.

> Why only six possible values per color channel? If each channel had seven possible values, the different combinations would result in 343 colors (7^3) — more than the 256 possible values in 8-bit color.

As technology becomes more sophisticated, there is growing debate over the need for Web-safe color. It is interesting to note that some newer computers and monitors no longer offer an 8-bit (256-color) display setting. The paradigm is certainly changing and we will eventually reach the point where this discussion is unnecessary. Better technology is now available for less money, and older computers with less video capability are moving off of desktops and into museums.

Despite the hopes of manufacturers, however, computers are not disposable — they have a useful life of more than a few months. Keep in mind that you're not designing only for other graphics professionals. Many businesses, schools, and individuals still have older technology, which means they won't be able to see the subtle color variations in your Website backgrounds.

When will this change?

That question is difficult to answer. No single thing will force a universal computer upgrade. The latest operating systems (both Macintosh OS X and Windows XP) are certainly driving forces, because the system software — and the applications that require it — take more power and memory than is available in older machines.

In addition, computers are still expensive. You can buy a small system for a few hundred dollars; this may seem like nothing to some, but it's more than a week's paycheck for others. Multiplied by the hundreds or thousands of systems used in business or school settings, upgrading to newer machines might cost millions of dollars.

When you design in color, you should consider not only what you are designing, but also who you are designing it for. If your audience is primarily graphic designers, you can assume most viewers will be able to see millions of colors. If you are designing a business-to-business site, you're probably safe with (at least) thousands of colors, but use them with caution.

If you are designing a site for the general consumer market, stick with Web-safe color until reputable statistics justify a change. It is arrogant to ignore low-end users simply because they have not chosen (or been able) to upgrade to newer computers.

Conclusion

To achieve the best possible output — whether for print or electronic media — you need to understand the nature of digital color capture and display. The quality of reproduction is affected by a number of factors, including the type of image, capture technology, color depth, resolution, file format, and intended output. The information presented here will be fundamental to any image you work with. In the next chapter, you will learn how these concepts apply to preparing output for color printing.

CHAPTER 5

Printing Color

As a mechanical process, color printing has inherent variations and limitations. The ease with which we create and apply colors in design software is deceptive. Although it is simple enough to place a color image or create a colored line in an electronic file, you always need to consider the final output goal to ensure that the color displayed on your monitor can be reproduced as you intend. There is a saying that the end justifies the means; when it comes to color reproduction, however, the end *defines* the means. You need to understand the process of commercial printing to be able to prepare your files correctly for optimum color representation.

Basic Press Mechanics

In process-color printing, the four process colors — cyan, magenta, yellow, and black (CMYK) — are imaged or separated onto individual printing plates. Each color separation is printed on a separate unit of a printing press. The semitransparent inks, when printed on top of each other in varying percentages, produce the range of colors in the CMYK gamut. Special (spot) colors are printed using specifically formulated inks as additional color separations.

A printing press can print one color of ink for each unit of the press. Process-color printing requires a four-unit printing press (modern presses range from one to eight or more units) to print all colors at once; alternatively, paper can be run twice through a two-color press to print all four colors, or (in very rare cases) four times through a one-color press. To reproduce CMYK images, each of the four process colors is screened independently.

To print each color, ink is fed from the press ink fountain to a roller. When the ink roller contacts the printing plate, ink adheres to the image areas of the printing plate. The ink is then transferred to a blanket and then to the substrate (in offset lithography), or directly to the substrate (in flexography and gravure).

A full color image is separated into cyan, magenta, yellow, and black components to be printed.

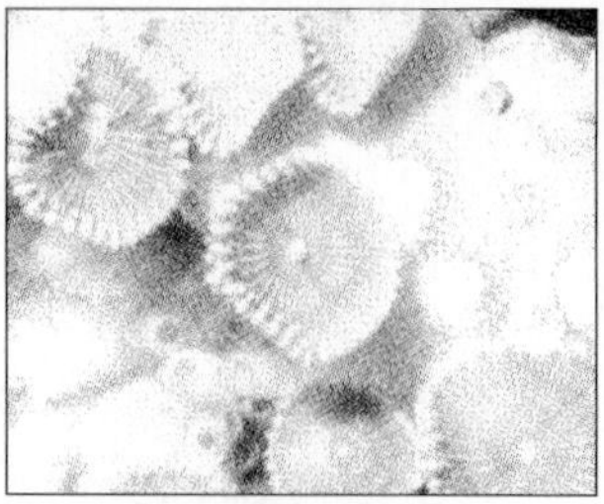

Cyan Separation

Magenta Separation

Yellow Separation

Black Separation

In a single-sided printing press, an impression cylinder provides the pressure necessary to transfer the ink to the substrate. Presses that print both sides of the sheet at once (called "perfecting presses") are configured so the two blanket cylinders — one for each side of the sheet — provide the required pressure.

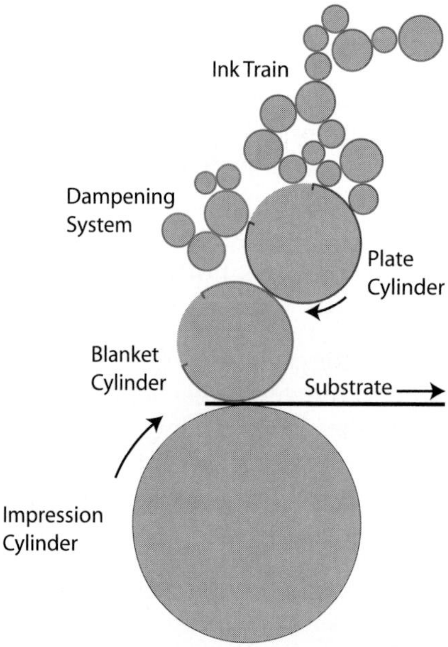

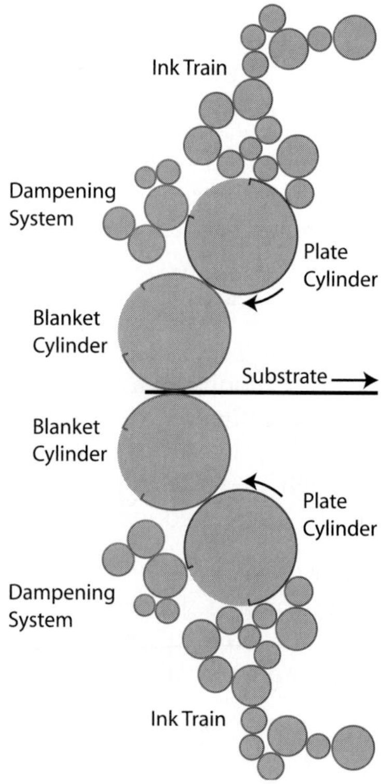

In a standard lithographic printing unit (left), the substrate passes between the blanket and impression cylinders. In a perfecting press (right), the substrate passes between the blanket cylinders of two printing units.

Understanding Halftones

Although your designs might incorporate continuous-tone photographs and other complex digital images, a printing press cannot print shades of color. Printing is a binary process — ink is either printed or not printed at a given location. To create the illusion of continuous tone, images are converted to halftone dots (a process called "screening").

To reproduce a photograph on a printing press, the image information recorded as pixels must be converted into a series of equally spaced, different-sized dots that fool the eye into believing that it sees continuous tones. The result of this conversion process is a "halftone image"; the dots that are used to simulate continuous tone are called "halftone dots." Light tones in a photograph are represented as small halftone dots; dark tones become large, overlapping halftone dots.

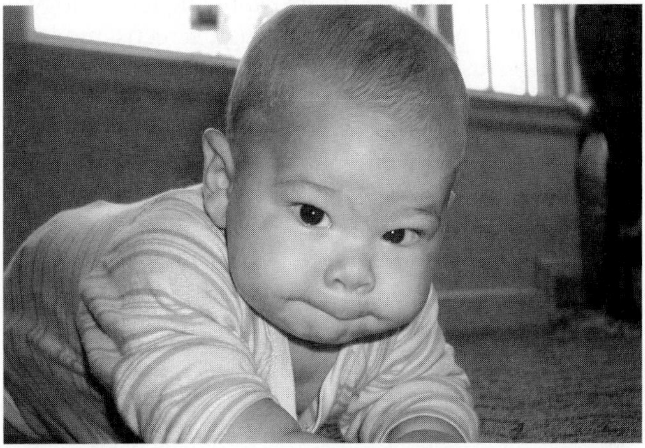

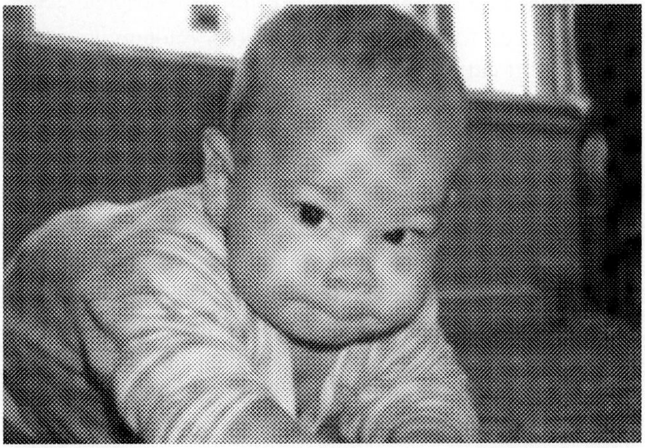

The bottom image shows simulated halftone dots for the sake of illustration; these dots are much larger than those used to create an actual halftone.

SCREEN RULING

Prior to the availability of image-editing software, photos were converted to halftones with large graphic-arts cameras and fine mesh screens. A picture was photographed through a screen to create halftone dots; different screens produced different numbers of dots in an inch, hence the term "dots per inch" (dpi).

The finite number of available dots in a horizontal or vertical inch of the screen through which it was photographed defined the *screen ruling* — sometimes called the "line screen" or "lines per inch" (lpi) — of the halftone. In every square inch of an image with a 133-lpi screen ruling, there are 133 × 133 (17,689) possible locations for a halftone dot. Decreasing the screen ruling results in fewer halftone dots and grainier images; increasing the screen ruling results in more halftone dots and clearer and more detailed images.

Although modern image capturing technology no longer involves photographing images through screens, modern presses still generate images using halftones, so it's still important to know what line screen will be used to prepare each specific job you work on. You can't just randomly select a line screen — it's a finite number based on a combination of the intended output device and the type of paper that will be used to print the job. Before you create your images, ask your service provider and printer what line screen will be used for your job. If you can't find out ahead of time, or are unsure, follow these general guidelines (from GRACoL):

> General Requirements for Applications in Commercial Offset Lithography (GRACoL), currently in version 6.0, is the collaborative result of a committee formed by the Graphic Communications Association. The committee was established in 1996 to develop a document containing general guidelines and recommendations that could be used as a reference source across the industry for quality color printing. Supported by the International Prepress Association and the Graphic Arts Technical Foundation, GRACoL has become a *de facto* standard for the industry.

- Newspaper or newsprint: 85–100 lpi
- Magazine or general commercial printing: 133–150 lpi
- Premium-quality-paper jobs (such as art books or annual reports): 150–175 lpi (some specialty jobs may use up to 200 lpi)

RESOLUTION REQUIREMENTS

In our discussion of images in Chapter 4, we defined resolution in terms of pixels per inch (ppi). When we discuss output resolution, we use some new terms in addition to ppi — "lines per inch" ("lpi"), "dots per inch" ("dpi"), and sometimes "spots per inch" ("spi").

- **Lines per inch (lpi)**. This measure is the number of halftone dots produced in a horizontal or vertical linear inch by a high-resolution imagesetter in order to simulate the appearance of continuous-tone color.
- **Dots per inch (dpi) or spots per inch (spi)**. This measure is the number of dots produced by an output device in a single line of output. This term is sometimes incorrectly used interchangeably with "pixels per inch."

Each halftone dot is created by calculating the average value of a group of pixels and generating a spot of ink of an appropriate size. An image's resolution defines the quantity of pixel data that the printer can read; images must have sufficient resolution to enable the output device to generate enough halftone dots to create the appearance of continuous tone.

Ideally, the printer should have four pixels for each halftone dot created. The relationship between pixels and halftone dots defines the rule of resolution for all raster-based images — the resolution of an image should be around two times the screen ruling that will be used for printing.

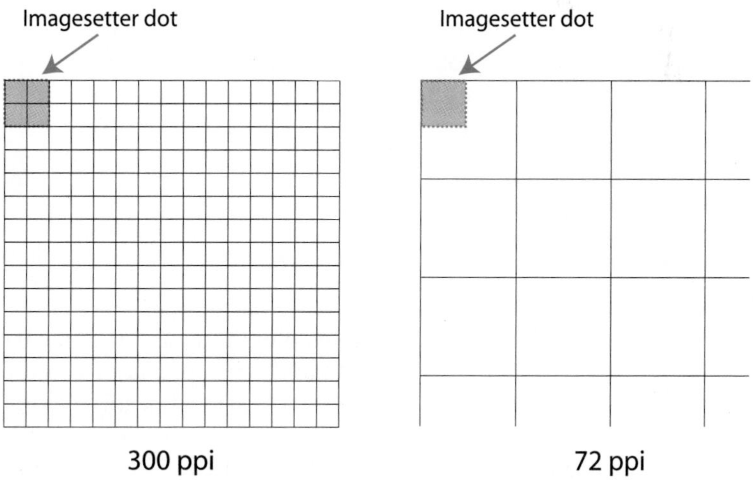

Each white square symbolizes a pixel in a digital image. The colored area shows the pixel information that is used to generate a halftone dot or spot. If an image only has 72 pixels per inch, the output device has to generate four halftone dots per pixel, resulting in poor printed image quality.

The same raster image is reproduced here at 300 ppi (left) and 72 ppi (right). Notice the obvious degradation in quality when the resolution is set to 72 ppi.

SCREEN ANGLES

Each color separation for an image will have the same line screen but a different *screen angle*. Ideally, the screen angles for each ink should be at 30° intervals. Obviously, this is not possible with four (process) ink colors, because the fourth ink would be equal to the first; to work around the problem, process inks are usually set at the following screen angles:

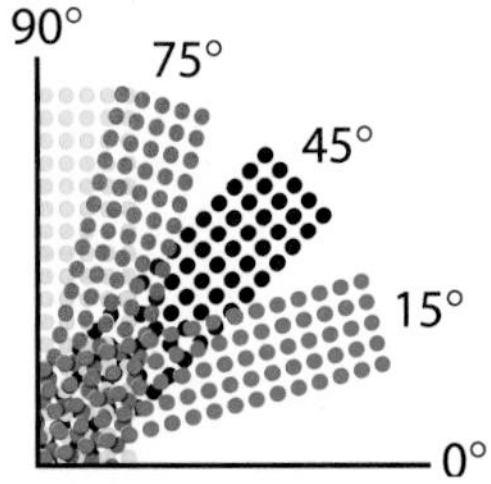

The grid of halftone dots for each color separation is rotated at a different screen angle.

Cyan =15°

Black = 45°

Magenta = 75°

Yellow = 0° (90°)

Black, the most noticeable color, is set at 45° since it is the least noticeable angle. Magenta and cyan inks are rotated 30° from the black screen angle; yellow, the least noticeable color, is rotated 15° from the magenta angle. These screen angles will create a rosette pattern when all four inks are printed. Any variation will typically result in a more objectionable pattern called "moiré," which will diminish the quality of the job.

Spot-Color Screen Angles

If you add spot colors to a process job, the spot-color screen angles are typically set to match the magenta screen angle. With multiple spot

Moiré is a visible pattern created by screen angles. When the black separation is set to 90° — the most visible angle — the moiré pattern becomes pronounced as seen in the image on the right.

colors, the darkest spot color is set to the magenta angle, the next darkest spot color is set to the cyan angle, and the third darkest color is set to the yellow screen angle. The same principle applies when building a job using only spot colors instead of process; in this case, however, you would assign the darkest spot-color angle to the black (45°) angle, and continue from the darkest to the lightest color.

FM Screening

Halftone images with consistent screen pattern and angle are created with a process commonly called "amplitude-modulated (AM) screening." The frequency and pattern of dots remain the same while the size of dots varies to create different levels of darkness.

Frequency-modulated (FM) screening, also called "stochastic screening," is a digital screening technique that does not use an assigned line screen or angle to create halftone dots. Rather, dots of equal (very small) size are placed quasi-randomly; shadow areas of an image have many dots close together while highlight areas have few or no dots.

FM screening eliminates the potential for moiré because there is no regular line screen and no conflicting screen angles. This benefit also makes FM screening popular for six-color printing technologies such as Hexachrome.

DOT GAIN

If you put a drop of paint on a piece of paper, the dot will spread out as the moisture is absorbed into the paper. This concept, called "dot gain" or "tone value increase," is an inherent part of the printing process. Each tiny halftone dot on a printing plate holds a spot of ink, which is transferred to paper as it moves through the press. When the wet ink contacts paper, the dot naturally spreads out to some degree.

This can become a problem if, for example, a 50% dot spreads out to become a 70% dot — any areas that should look like 50% of the color will look like 70% of the color. Obviously, this causes images to appear very dark, and compromises detail in the shadowed areas. Dot gain can cause significant variation from the color you specify.

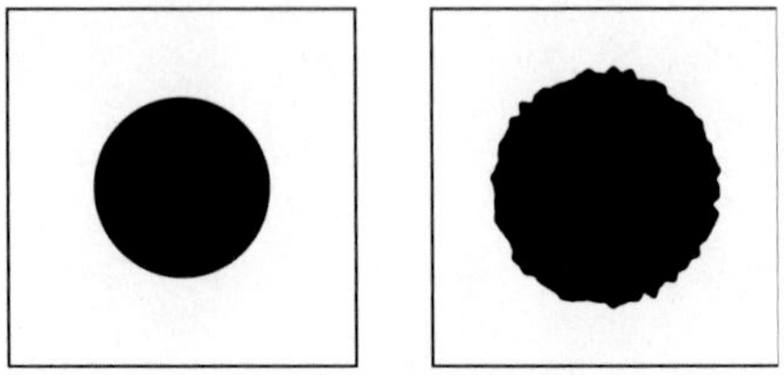

A 50% dot on the printing plate (left) can gain to a 70% dot when printed (right).

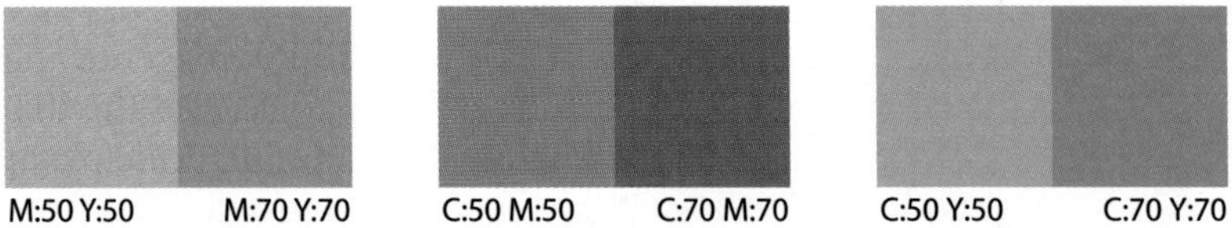

If a defined 50% dot gains to 70% on press, the job colors will appear very different than what you expect.

The amount of expected dot gain varies depending on the specific line screen, ink, paper, and press used for a job. The best way to know exactly what to expect is to run a press test using the same consumables as your final job. In most cases, commercial printers do exactly this; they are well aware of the potential problems caused by dot gain, and they keep libraries of data for specific ink/paper/press combinations. Most commercial printers will be able to provide you with a dot-gain profile for your job, which you can use when creating CMYK separations for your images.

If you put a dot of paint between two sheets of paper and press down, the dot would spread out even farther because of the applied pressure. The same concept is true with printing. The problem of dot gain is exacerbated by the pressure between the blanket cylinder and impression cylinder, which must be carefully monitored. If the pressure between the two cylinders is too high, the printed dot can be "smashed" or spread out beyond what is expected and compensated for.

INK-FILM THICKNESS

The amount of ink transferred from each printing unit is called "ink-film thickness." To understand how ink-film thickness affects color, think of painting a picture with watercolors. The more paint you apply to the paper, the darker the final color will be. The same is true of printing ink — a thicker ink film produces a darker color. High ink-film thickness in one or more of the process inks can also cause the hue and saturation to shift, resulting in a color other than what you may have expected or intended. Higher ink-film thickness also increases dot gain.

To monitor ink-film thickness and dot gain, printers add a color bar to the edge of the press sheet. This color bar is usually outside the trim area of the job, but is sometimes placed in an area that will not affect the final appearance of the product. If you look at the inside flap of a cereal box, for example, you might see blocks of different colors in different percentages.

A color bar is not much more than a series of color patches in varying percentages. These can be purchased from a number of commercial vendors, but can also be created manually and added to the imposed file before film or plates are created. (Some commercial color bars include target elements such as stars and checkerboards to facilitate evaluation and detection of dot gain problems.)

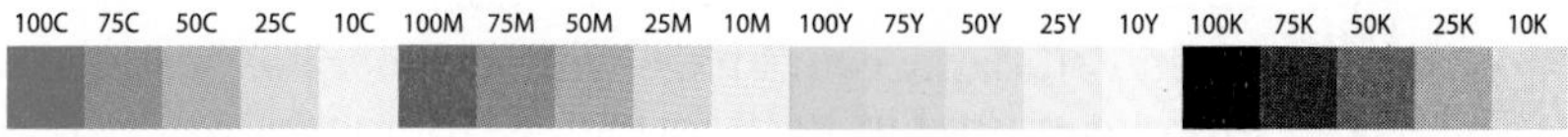

When the job is being printed, the color patches in the bar provide a known target for the press operator to match during *makeready*, which is the process of starting the press and manipulating the controls until it is running at its optimum capabilities. (This is similar to turning on a faucet on a cold morning and waiting for the water to get warm…your shower makeready.) After the press is "up to color," the color bar is then used to monitor and maintain ideal press conditions throughout the press run.

> Printers typically use a densitometer or spectrophotometer to measure the ink-film thickness of color bar patches. This helps to remove the subjective element of color printing.

PRINTABLE DOTS AND INK COVERAGE

To accurately reproduce highlights and shadows on a commercial printing press, you need to understand the concept of minimum printable dot and maximum printable dot. A 1% dot, for example, is so small that the mechanical aspects of the printing process cause anything specified as a 1% dot to *drop out* (not print at all), resulting in highlights that lack detail and contrast. The minimum *printable* dot, then, is the smallest size dot that can be faithfully and consistently reproduced. The Specifications for Web Offset Publications (SWOP) indicate 5% as the minimum printable dot, although some printers specify a dot as small as 3%.

The *total area coverage* (TAC), also called "total ink density," is the largest percentage of ink that can be safely printed in a single area. The paper's absorption rate, speed of the printing press, and other mechanical factors limit the amount of ink that can be placed on the same area of the substrate. If too much ink is printed, the result is a dark blob with no visible detail; heavy layers of ink also result in drying problems, smearing, and a number of other issues.

Although the concept may sound complex, TAC can be easily calculated by adding the percentages of each ink used in the printing process. If a color is defined as C:45 M:60 Y:90 K:0, the total area coverage is 195% (45 + 60 + 90 + 0).

The total area coverage limit varies according to the ink/paper/press combination used for a given job. SWOP indicates a 300% maximum. According to the GRACoL publication, maximum TAC limits are between 240% and 320% for offset lithography. Many sheetfed printers require 280% maximum, while the number for newspapers is usually around 240% because the lower-quality paper absorbs more ink.

Preparing Color for Print

When you digitize an image with a camera or scanner, it is almost always captured in RGB format. RGB images will look okay in the page-layout document, and will even print to a composite color printer; however, when color separations are output, as required for print reproduction, all the image information in RGB images might end up on the black plate. It's important to remember that the RGB space is not useful for commercial printing — you need to convert RGB colors and images to the CMYK process model. The following section describes procedures for creating colors in the CMYK color space, and for working with special (spot) colors, both of which are acceptable for commercial printing.

> Some output devices (PostScript Level 3) offer in-RIP conversion capability, which means all RGB images will be converted to CMYK "on-the-fly" based on the current settings in the output device. This does free you from worrying about converting individual images, but does not provide the image-by-image control many designers prefer. You will also not be able to monitor the color shift that results from the conversion.

COLOR BY NUMBERS

Developing a comfortable understanding of the physical printing process gives you a distinct advantage in correctly preparing colors in your files. Keeping in mind that your ultimate goal is to accurately reproduce the color of an original subject using CMYK inks, your first task is to determine how to define that color in the electronic files that you create. Many beginning designers make the mistake of basing color choices on what they see on their monitors — and they're frequently disappointed when the blue skies they create don't look right when they're printed with process-color inks. Even if you have calibrated your monitor, no monitor is 100% effective at simulating printed color. As long as monitors display color in the RGB color space, there will always be some discrepancies.

Defining Process Colors

To determine the exact color you want to create, you need to use a *densitometer*, which measures the amount of light reflected from a surface. A light with known color properties is directed onto the surface to be measured. The densitometer analyzes the light that is reflected, calculates the light that was absorbed, and returns the value of ink percentages necessary to create the specific color. If you want to match a color that has already been printed, you should use a spectrophotometer or a hardware densitometer to determine the ink build of the color. Some graphics applications include a software densitometer, which shows you the CMYK ink percentages defined in any specific pixel or selection.

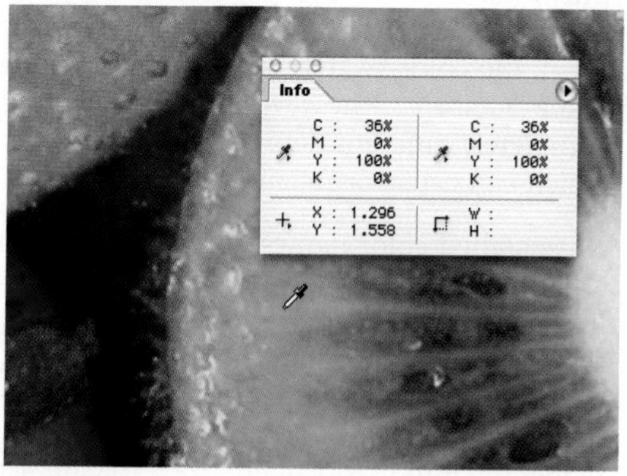

Photoshop includes an Eyedropper tool that provides the RGB and CMYK values of any pixel in an image. Use these values to determine color results; don't rely on what you see on the screen.

When designing for print, the most important point to remember is that you should use *numbers* — not what you see on your screen — to designate your color choices. As you do this more often, you will become better able to predict the outcome for a given process-ink build. Rely on what you *know* to be true rather than what you *hope* will be.

Once you determine the CMYK percentages assigned to a particular pixel, you can look up those values in a *process-color chart* to view a pre-printed swatch that will show exactly how the color will appear on press. Every serious designer should have some sort of process-color chart, which are available from several commercial publishers; some printers can even provide charts produced on the exact press your job will be printed on. These process-color charts (or swatch books) contain little squares of process-ink builds so you can see, for example, what a process build of C:10 M:70 Y:30 K:20 will look like when printed. These guides usually show samples in steps of 5% or 10%, printed on both coated and uncoated paper (because the type of *substrate* can dramatically affect the final print quality).

> When designing for print, the most important point to remember is that you should use *numbers* — not what you see on your screen — to designate your color choices. As you do this more often, you will become better able to predict the outcome for a given process-ink build. Rely on what you *know* to be true rather than what you *hope* will be.

Naming Process Colors

If a designer uses a color swatch when creating an image with an illustration program, and then imports that image into a layout application, there is the possibility that color names could be mismatched. For example, a designer could define Color #1 as C:50 Y:75 in QuarkXPress; an Illustrator EPS file from another designer defines Color #1 as M:77 Y:80 K:15. When the Illustrator file is placed into the Quark document, the color-swatch name is also imported into the layout file. The name "Color #1," however, is already used in the layout file with a completely different definition. The result is a *mismatched color name*, which can cause problems in the output process.

Mismatched color names occur when the same color name has two different definitions — one defined in the page layout and one defined in a placed image file. When the files are output, the RIP may be confused by different definitions for the same color name; the imported value might replace the layout document's value for that particular color name (or vice versa). The change could be subtle, or it could be drastic.

> Adobe InDesign includes a feature that automatically names new colors according to their content, which suggests that the industry is approaching an accepted standard convention.

This problem is common if you are dealing with a layout file that includes contributions from more than one designer — for example, a magazine layout that includes files from multiple advertisers. Each designer might assign completely different CMYK values to a color called "Border." When both of those images are imported into the same layout file, the two different colors have the same name of "Border," and the output device does not know which to use.

> Using names such as "new swatch" or "border color" will cause trouble later in the printing process. You should always use a standard naming convention that is based on the color content.

There is no standard for naming colors, so we recommend using some meaningful sequence that reflects the color content. For example, "C75 M50 Y0 K0" is much more precise than "Medium Blue" — there are many shades of Medium Blue, but only one ink combination defined by C75 M50 Y0 K0. This naming convention serves two purposes:

- If you name the color by the CMYK values, you are more likely to remember that the colors in your documents need to actually be CMYK values.
- You know exactly what the color contains, so you can easily see if you duplicate colors.

Defining Spot Colors

Spot colors are frequently used in the graphics industry to produce a special look, to match an exact color, or to highlight a certain aspect of a job with varnish or a special coating. Spot-color inks are opaque, so they produce the desired result with a single printing unit instead of by combining varying percentages of the four process inks.

If you want a certain look, or a color that must be the same on every printed job, spot colors are usually the best choice. Of course, adding spot color to a process job does add to the cost, and budgets are usually a consideration when designing a print project. Many projects that make use of spot colors will cross your desk — colors can be designed for foil stamping, varnish plates, highly saturated colors, and other special considerations.

> Spot colors are commonly used for corporate identity and packaging, or any other application for which brand recognition is important. Coca-Cola, for example, has a specially formulated red ink that is used on all of the company's products. In this case, brand identity is so closely linked to the color that the company holds a copyright on the ink formula.

Conversely, using spot colors can sometimes help to *reduce* the cost of a job. Combining a single spot color with black is a common way to create high-quality, professional results at far less cost than a four-color process job. Two-color jobs also allow you to create *duotone* images, which add contrast and interest to layouts. Annual reports, catalogs, books, and corporate identity pieces are all good candidates for two-color printing.

Spot colors need to be defined before they can be used in layout or illustration programs. Most graphics-software applications come with color libraries — digital swatches from which you can select spot colors. Because libraries of PANTONE swatches, for example, are built into most graphics software, you don't have to define a PANTONE ink before using it in an illustration. PANTONE colors are specific ink formulas, and their definitions are built in along with the swatches.

In addition to a process-color chart, every designer should also have a set of spot-color guides, such as the ones produced for the PANTONE Matching System (PMS). PANTONE, Trumatch, Focoltone, and other systems all have printed guides so designers can look through swatches and select the exact color they want the final work to use. The special-color guides also usually show coated and uncoated samples; some show the process-color combination that produces the closest possible match to the spot ink. If you want to approximate a special-ink color, you can use those ink percentages to designate the process color in a layout or illustration program.

> Before you begin a job using special-ink systems, ask your printer which system their company uses; if they use Trumatch and you designate PANTONE colors, you might have problems getting the job printed the way you want it.

Naming Spot Colors

When you specify spot colors in a page-layout, illustration, or image file, you should leave the name of the color as it appears when you choose it from the software library. Changing the name of spot inks could introduce problems into the production process.

For example, a designer selects PANTONE 270 CVU spot color in Quark, and names the color "Border color"; another designer selects the same PANTONE color in FreeHand, but names the swatch "Spec Blue." When the FreeHand illustration is placed into the Quark document, two different spot-color plates will separate during printing even though the different color names refer to the same PANTONE ink.

A similar problem can occur when you select PANTONE colors from built-in software libraries. When you specify PANTONE colors in a layout or image, you will notice there are several different libraries to choose from — and several of the libraries have very similar names.

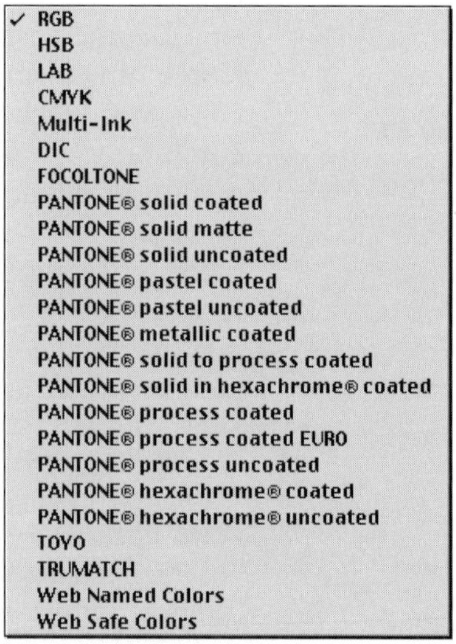

Before you choose a color from a library, you first have to choose which library to use. The name of the selected color shows the number, followed by one or more letters that indicate which library you used.

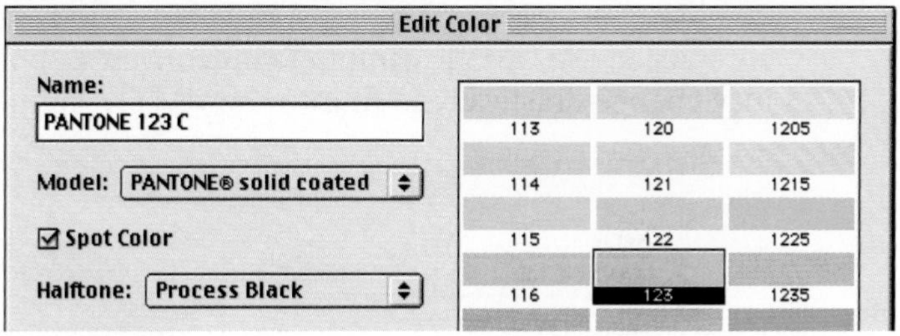

A PANTONE color name shows the number of the specified ink, followed by an extension to indicate the specific library you are using.

The various PANTONE libraries each append a different letter combination after the number, but any two colors that have the same number are printed using the same ink. The distinction between the Solid Coated and Solid Uncoated libraries is only evident when you look at the printed swatch books, which show the result of the same color ink printed on coated and uncoated paper.

A problem often arises when you choose the same ink color, but from different libraries. If, for example, you choose PANTONE 123 C in a page layout, then import a duotone image that specifies PANTONE 123 U, the file will output two unique separations — one for each version of PANTONE 123 — instead of one. When you prepare a color job for printing, pay close attention to PANTONE colors with the same numbers but different letters; these are likely to be errors that must be fixed before you print the job.

CONVERTING BETWEEN COLOR MODELS

If you are working on a job that is intended to be only a four-color job, then you need to convert all colors and color elements to process colors before printing. Using the incorrect color space is a common error found in print jobs. Many designers forget to convert RGB images; others neglect to change spot colors defined in a layout or vector graphic. Failing to convert RGB images can result in faulty separations — in most cases, all of the information will separate only to the black plate. If you don't change all spot colors to process colors, the printer will generate an additional color separation plate for each spot color used in the page.

In most graphics software, you can change a spot color to its nearest process equivalent by simply unchecking a Spot Color check box. Because we are advocating a standardized color-naming convention, though, we encourage you to change the name of spot colors accordingly when you change color models.

Be aware that when you convert spot colors to their process equivalents, sometimes the resultant colors are different if the spot color is outside the possible gamut for process inks; this is called "color shift."

One possible reason for using spot colors is to reproduce colors that are outside the CMYK gamut; if you convert a spot color to process, it may change drastically to fit into the CMYK gamut.

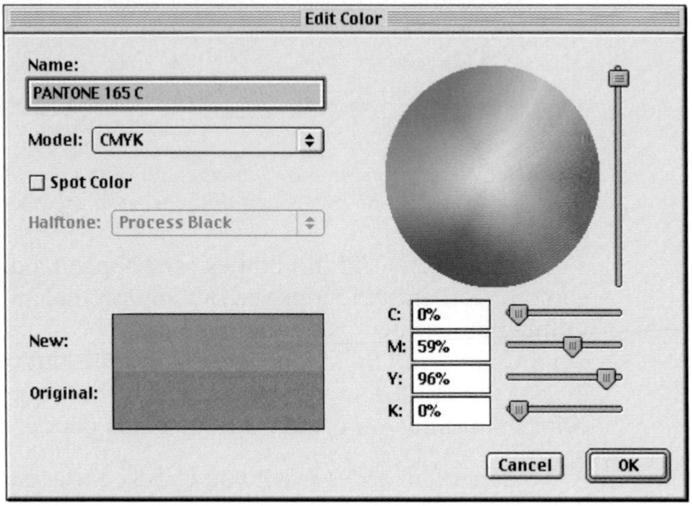

If you change a color from PANTONE to CMYK, you can expect a different color to print. The Edit Color dialog box in QuarkXPress shows digital swatches of the original and new colors, which gives you an idea of how the color will shift.

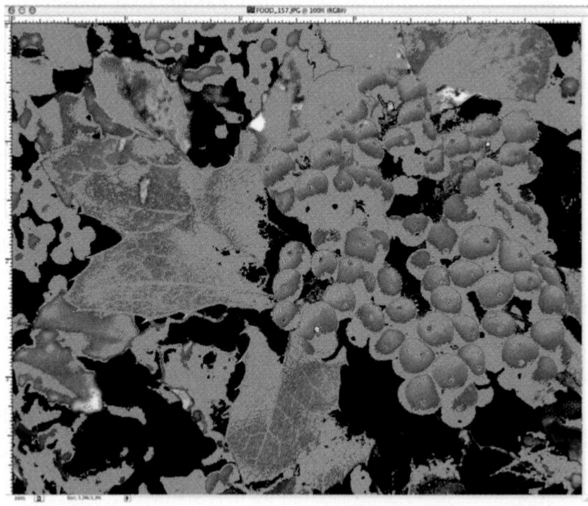

In Photoshop, you can preview an image to find which colors are outside the CMYK gamut. Any colors appearing in gray will be compressed into the CMYK gamut once converted for printing.

Images with Spot Colors

If you intend to print with spot colors, you can embed them directly into an image by creating additional channels in an image-editing application such as Photoshop. Each spot-color channel in an image file will produce an additional separation, whether the image is printed independently or placed into a page-layout document.

In Photoshop, for example, you can add a spot channel to an RGB or CMYK image. If you add the spot channel to an RGB image, the spot channel is not affected when you convert RGB to CMYK. For documents in the CMYK model, anything you draw, type, place, or create on the spot channel will be output to a fifth separation when the file is printed.

> When you place an image with a spot-color channel into a page-layout document, the spot color is added to the application's Color palette for the document you are using.

Adding a spot channel to a color image is especially useful if you are using an image-editing application to create an entire document, such as a postcard or flyer. This technique allows you to incorporate logos or other identity spot colors into an otherwise process-color job. You can also use spot channels to add varnish or special coatings to selected areas of an image, which can create some unique special effects in an otherwise two-dimensional medium.

To save Photoshop images with spot channels in Photoshop, you have to use the DCS2 file format. (You can also save spot channels in the native Photoshop format, but those files can't be placed into some page-layout documents.)

Multichannel and Duotone Images

There are two additional options for creating images with spot colors: duotones and multichannel images. A *duotone* is an image reproduced with only two colors of ink, usually black and one additional spot color. Shadows are reproduced as shades of black, and midtones are reproduced in the second color. (You can also create *tritones* with three ink colors or *quadtones* with four ink colors.) This type of image is commonly used to add visual interest to two-color printing jobs.

Converting a grayscale image to a duotone can add visual interest if you are printing with two ink colors.

Manipulating the second color in a duotone can produce unique effects with only two ink colors.

Although this is not a book about Photoshop, you should be aware that you can manipulate the appearance of the different ink colors used in a duotone (or tritone or quadtone), which changes the appearance of the entire image — either subtly or drastically. Duotones must be saved in the EPS format.

In a *multichannel image*, you create and define each channel individually. This is useful for specialty printing applications, such as printing two spot colors and a varnish or printing only specific areas or elements in color. If you create multichannel images in Photoshop, you have to save them in the DCS2 format. Using Multichannel mode, you have more control over the content of each channel than you do using duotones.

BUILDING COLOR GRADIENTS

Gradients (also called "vignettes," "blends," or "graduated fills") are created with a series of bands. *Banding* results when those individual bands are visible, rather than shifting smoothly from one step to the next. Banding is listed in GRACoL as the second biggest problem associated with printing digital files, behind only incorrect or missing fonts.

One of the problems with gradients is that they are so easy to create. Practically every application used for graphics, image editing, or layout allows you to create gradients with virtually no restriction. The technical aspects of the printing process, however, do not allow some of the gradients that designers create to be reproduced.

Calculating Gradients

Specific formulas govern the number of gray levels that can be reproduced for a given printing process; if a gradient contains more gray levels than the output device can create, banding results.

The following series of calculations allows you to make sure that a blend will print without banding. (You will need your calculator for this. Unfortunately, there is no software program to do this for you; if there were, banding might be less of a problem.)

Step 1. (Resolution of the output device [dpi] ÷ line screen [lpi])^2 + 1 = Number of possible gray levels

Note: Drop anything after the decimal point; only use the integer value of the calculation. Also, the number of possible gray levels should not exceed 256, because most RIPs can only reproduce 256 levels.

Step 2. Number of possible gray levels x % change in blend = Number of possible tints for the blend

Step 3. Length of blend ÷ Number of possible tints for the blend = Size of each band

Using these formulas, you can create a blend that will not show banding. For example, consider a 5-in. blend that begins at 25% black and blends to 95% black. The final output will be on a 2540-dpi filmsetter using a 150-line screen. The formula applies:

Step 1. $(2540 \div 150)^2 + 1 = 287$ possible gray levels

(Because 256 is the maximum number of gray shades, discard anything greater than 256.)

Step 2. $256 \times (95\% - 25\%) = 256 \times 70\% = 256 \times 0.70 =$ 179.2 possible tints

Multiply the length of the blend by 72 to convert the measurement from inches to points. (There are 72 points in one inch.)

Step 3. 360 pt. ÷ 179.2 = 2.0089 pt. for each gray level in the blend

According to Adobe, any blend with bands less than 3 points wide will not show noticeable banding. This particular combination, then, will work.

Troubleshooting Gradients

This seems like a lot of math for something so easily executed in a software application. However, remember that banding is the second biggest problem encountered in digital production. If you want to avoid the problem, do the math. You can also use a few simple guidelines to help reduce banding:

- **Increase the resolution of the output device.** More resolution gives you more gray levels to work with.
- **Decrease the line-screen ruling.** As a factor in determining the possible gray levels, lower screen ruling allows more gray levels.

As a designer, however, you probably have no choice about resolution or screen ruling. If that is the case, you can decrease the likelihood of banding by adhering to the following rules:

- **Keep gradients short.** The longer the gradient, the larger individual bands will be and the more likely they will show.
- **Use a larger color range in the blend.** A 20% difference is much more likely to band than a 70% difference.
- **Add noise.** Try recreating the gradient in Photoshop and adding a small amount of noise. The noise will be virtually imperceptible to the eye, but will create enough variation so the bands will appear smooth when printed.

The top gradient has a 30% difference in color between the beginning and end points. It is far more likely to show banding than the bottom gradient, which has a 100% difference between start and end points.

Understanding Registration

Because printing is a mechanical process, some variation between the different units of the press is possible (if not likely). Paper moves through the units of a press at considerable speed, and some movement from side to side is inevitable. To counter the effects of this movement, each printing plate has one or more *registration marks* (crosshairs) that are used to monitor the registration (or alignment) of each color. If the units are in register, the crosshairs from each color plate will print exactly on top of each other.

When a press is out of register, the individual colors are discernible.

For many reasons — the mechanics of the movement of paper through the stations of the offset press, paper shrinkage or expansion, and so on — the position of one or more of the four printing plates may be out of register by some amount. Although usually quite small, this slight *misregister* can cause a noticeable gap of uninked paper between adjacent elements, particularly when these elements are made up of different ink colors.

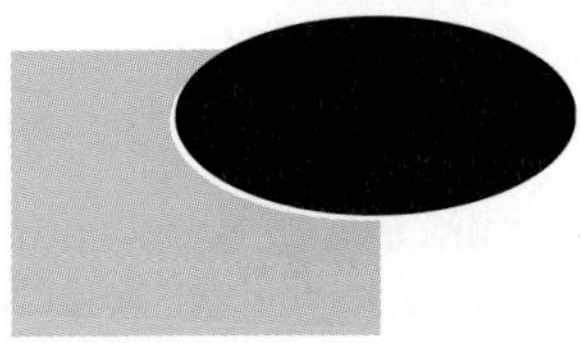

Misregister can result in a thin but visible gap between two objects.

If any misregister occurs on press, type can become blurry or, worse, virtually unreadable. Any time multiple ink colors are placed on top of each other, you run the risk of misregister.

Misregister

Misregister

Even slight misregister will blur the sharp edges of type, especially thin serifs as in this Minion font.

TRAPPING

> As a general rule, small type and type with thin serifs should not be printed with more than one color of ink.

Trapping is the compensation for misregister of the color plates on a printing press. Trapping minimizes or eliminates these errors by artificially expanding adjacent colors so that small areas of color on the edge of each element overlap and print on top of one another. If sufficiently large, this expansion of color, or *trap*, fills in the undesirable inkless gap between elements.

> If you are a designer, you may never have to touch the trapping controls in your graphic-design software. Remember this rule: ask your service provider whether they want you to apply trapping, and, if so, what settings you should use. Many service providers and printers have high-end solutions that apply trapping to your documents. If they do, any trap settings that you make in your software will be overwritten.

Trapping procedures differ based upon workflow; most service providers will perform trapping before generating film or plates. The specific amount of trapping to be applied varies, depending on the ink/paper/press combination. Trapping is almost always applied at the printer's prepress department, but you should still be aware of the issue when you create artwork. There are a few things you can do to help minimize the chance of problems.

KNOCKOUTS AND OVERPRINTS

A *knockout* is an area of background color that is removed so a lighter foreground color is visible. To achieve white (paper-colored) type on a black background, for example, the black background is removed wherever the type overlaps the black. Any time a lighter color appears on top of a darker color, the area of the lighter color is knocked out of the background.

Overprinting is essentially the opposite of knockout. A darker-color foreground object is printed directly on top of a lighter-color background, which means that slight variation in the units of the press will not be as noticeable, especially if the darker color is entirely contained within the lighter color.

Obviously, overprinting only works for darker inks. Printing yellow ink on top of black ink, for example, will not be a terribly effective design solution. Black is commonly set to overprint other colors, as are some special colors that are printed with opaque inks. Black is particularly effective when overprinted because it becomes visually richer when other process colors — especially cyan — are mixed with it.

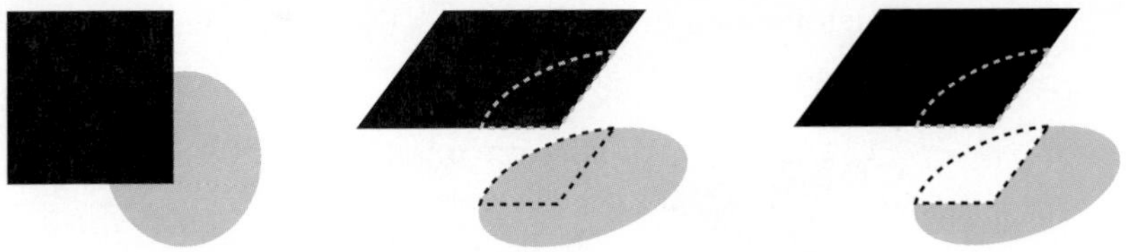

When a color is set to knock out, anything beneath that color will not be printed. If the black knocks out the cyan, any misregistration may result in a paper-colored gap where the two objects meet. Setting black to overprint eliminates the possibility of a gap caused by misregister. (The dashed lines in the graphic are for illustration only and will not print.)

RICH BLACKS

Designers frequently use *rich blacks* (or *superblacks*) to increase the density of the black. When specifying the color in a layout or illustration program, a percentage of cyan is added to 100% black to create a denser, cooler black; magenta added to 100% black creates a warmer black. People often describe rich blacks as looking "blacker."

Though rich blacks can visually enhance a design, they create a potential register problem for the press, especially when used for small type, thin lines, or rules. Avoid using rich blacks for these small elements unless the black is overprinting a larger area of another solid color. Also, limit rich blacks to two or three colors of ink. Some designers try to over-enhance solid blacks by adding percentages of all three process colors (CMY); this simply isn't necessary, and increases the possibility of registration problems.

COMMON COLORS

Using common color in adjacent elements is one way to avoid the possibility of a white gap between elements of an illustration or page. Using *common colors* means that two touching objects each have some percentage of the same process ink.

If adjacent elements share a large percentage of one or more common colors, then trapping between those elements is not necessary. If both elements contain a lot of magenta, for example, the continuity of the magenta between the two objects will mask any gaps that occur between the other process colors in the two images; this makes trapping unnecessary. The general rule is that if two adjacent elements share one process color that varies by less than 50%, or if the two elements share two or more process colors that vary by less than 80%, don't bother with trapping — the continuous layer of the inks common to both elements will effectively mask any gaps.

The following image illustrates this principle:

These two objects share magenta as a common color.
Because the color is printed in the shape of both objects combined, any shift in the cyan or yellow registration will not show a paper-colored gap.

CHOKES AND SPREADS

A *choke* means that the edge of the background color is expanded into the space in which the foreground color will be printed. A *spread* means that the edge of the *foreground* color is expanded to overprint the edge of the background color. As a general rule, the lighter object should be trapped into the darker area. This rule helps determine whether you should choke or spread.

- If the background is darker than the foreground object, the lighter color of the foreground object should be spread to overprint the darker background.
- If the foreground color is darker than the background color, the lighter background color should be choked to overprint the darker foreground color.

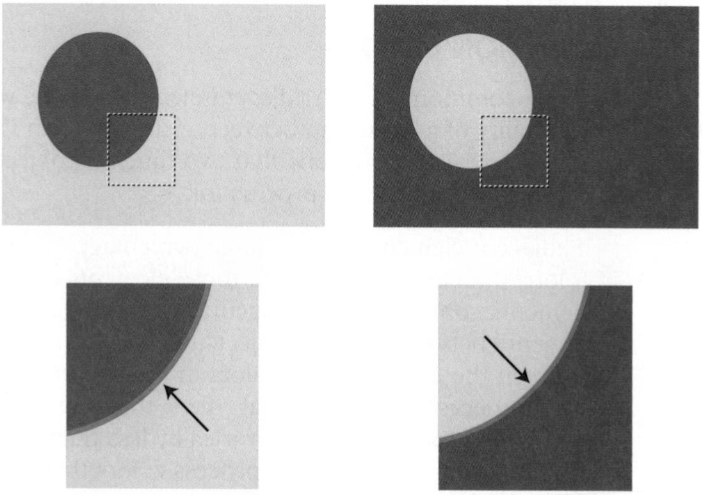

In the left image, the background color is choked into the darker foreground.
In the right image, the foreground circle is spread into the darker background.

TRAPPING TERMINOLOGY

Most graphic-design software offers the ability to trap color elements to some extent. In addition to application-based trapping, service bureaus and printers often use programs that are solely dedicated to trapping. These applications are powerful solutions for trapping complex files, and can usually handle more detailed trapping that is not available in layout and illustration software. Depending on the software you are using, trapping can be applied in a number of ways. The following section describes the general options for trapping.

Color-Specific Trapping

This type of trapping allows you to define the trapping behavior and amount for specific colors in a document. With color-specific trapping, you can define how each color is trapped to each other color. For example, you can set black to spread 0.25 pt. into magenta, spread 0.144 pt. into yellow, and overprint cyan. Each color defined in a document can have different defined trap settings relative to each other color in the same document.

When using color-specific trapping, you may also have the option to define color relationships as dependent or independent. Dependent trap settings automatically apply the inverse trap amount when the foreground/background relationship is reversed. In other words, if a black foreground spreads 0.25 pt. into a magenta background, a dependent trap setting means that a magenta foreground will be choked 0.25 pt. into a black background.

Item-Specific Trapping

This type of trapping allows you to control the trap behavior of individual elements in a document. Rather than defining trapping for individual colors, you can assign trap characteristics to specific objects in the document — text, lines, boxes, or other drawing (vector-based) elements. You can apply specific trapping settings to any object in a document except imported photos (raster images).

In some applications, you can apply trapping to only the part of an object that overlaps another object. When trapping partial overlaps, variable trap settings are applied to the top object in the stacking order where it overlaps other objects; edges of the top object that do not touch other areas of color are not affected.

Object-to-Image Trapping

The ability to trap an object created in the layout application against a bitmapped image imported from another document presents a complex trapping problem. The bitmapped image may be composed of a wide variety of different colors and densities, many of which are adjacent to the edge of the native object. Ideally, the program would calculate individual trapping values for each adjacent pixel and would not trap against white. In practice, however, the color in the native object is typically just spread to overprint adjacent areas of the imported image.

Object-to-Gradient Trapping

The ability to mask a gradient, particularly one gradient against another gradient, requires software to be capable of calculating trapping values for each of the individual incrementally colored objects. Few design applications feature trapping functions that can perform this feat; trapping gradients typically requires a dedicated trapping application such as Creo TrapWise.

Process Trapping

The individual separations of a document can be trapped separately. In other words, the cyan component of a foreground object is compared to the cyan component of the background object, the magenta component of a foreground object is compared to the magenta component of the background object, and so on.

HOW MUCH TO TRAP?

Unfortunately, as with so many other technical aspects of print design, there is no definitive answer to the question, "How much trapping should I use?" The required trap width varies based on a number of factors including the type of press used (sheetfed or web), the specific paper and ink used, the age and reliability of the press used, and so on. Before you apply trap settings in your design files, you should ask your printer or service provider what settings will work best for their equipment, or if they prefer that you do nothing so their staff can apply any necessary trapping.

Conclusion

There are obviously many issues to consider when you are creating or correcting files for color printing. The potential problems associated with color underscore the importance of understanding the printing process. Color separations, screen angles, inks, and press registration all contribute to the quality of your final printed work. If you don't have at least a fundamental understanding of these technical requirements, you cannot effectively prepare a job for printing.

CHAPTER 6

Color Management

Color management as a predictive tool has been around for decades, but nobody ever called it "color management." Before anyone ever heard of Photoshop, printers and color separators adjusted process-camera exposures, film chemistry, and later, drum scanners connected to film recorders to separate images according to the press conditions. The usual goal in color reproduction is to achieve an equivalent color appearance to the original by adjusting the reproduction for substrate and printing conditions. When you know the press conditions and have your systems running to a known target, you can be fairly sure your separations will look good.

Advances in computer and scanning technology drove color reproduction out of the specialty shops and onto the desktop. The type of color management that we discuss is a software-controlled system based on the specifications of the *International Color Consortium* (ICC), a standards body founded by leading manufacturers of software and hardware used in color reproduction.

Color Management Defined

A *color-management system* (CMS) is intended to preserve color fidelity and ensure predictability and consistency throughout the color-reproduction process. Monitors display color using additive RGB light, and most printers use subtractive CMYK inks or dyes — so files typically need to be translated into various color spaces as they move through the production workflow. Without color management, it's impossible to be certain that the colors displayed on the computer screen will match the colors that are printed.

In other words, a CMS can eliminate the ambiguity that arises when a color is only specified by some numbers. You might mix up a nice royal purple in a software program, but without color management, that same set of RGB numbers might look more lilac or lavender on another computer, or on paper when converted to CMYK for printing. A well-tuned CMS can translate the numbers that define a color in one color space to numbers that can better represent that color on another device.

If everything is set up correctly, ICC color management enables you to do three things with a high degree of confidence and predictability:

- Convert color images from one color space to another (e.g., from RGB to CMYK).
- See colors on a monitor as they will appear in print.
- Proof images on relatively inexpensive printers.

It's important to have realistic expectations of color management, and to realize that color management isn't a replacement for a thorough knowledge of the color-reproduction process. Even at its best, color management can't fix bad scans or bad photos — all it can do is provide consistency and predictability to a process that otherwise rarely has either.

A CMS helps maintain *apparent* color consistency across different types of media, such as a magazine that is both printed on a press and available on a Web site. We say "apparent" consistency because no technology exists yet that allows an image to look exactly the same in print, on photo paper, on a monitor, or on another type of physical medium such as a slide or a TV screen.

The bright, saturated colors of a slide, for example, are impossible to reproduce exactly on paper, but color management can help make sure that the same hues of color and apparent brightness and contrast are maintained. (Contrast can suffer tremendously when images are printed, so it's important to maintain the appearance of brightness and contrast.) Generally, it is saturation that suffers when an image is reproduced in print.

Color-management systems can also ensure that colors are visually consistent when the same product is printed in different locations or with different printing processes. For example, the North American edition of *National Geographic* magazine is printed on gravure presses, which have a large CMYK gamut. Regional editions in other languages, which have smaller print runs, are printed on offset lithographic presses, which have a smaller CMYK gamut. The term "visually consistent" does not guarantee identical output — the color-reproduction capabilities of such drastically different printing technologies make it impossible to achieve a perfect match. If you place examples of the same image printed by both gravure and offset side-by-side, the colors in both reproductions are consistent, but the image printed by offset lithography is less saturated and lighter overall than the one printed by gravure.

Another important use of color-management technology is to simulate various printing technologies (such as the newspaper-reproduction process) with the large gamut of an inkjet printer. The default settings of most inkjet printers often produce gorgeous, saturated prints that cannot be matched on any press, so you must explicitly set up a printer to simulate a particular printing press's reproduction capability (discussed in Chapter 8).

Apple's ColorSync and Microsoft's ICM (Image Color Matching) technologies are color-management systems that work at the operating-system level. Building the CMS into the operating systems gives programs such as Photoshop a way of performing consistent color-managed transformations using the color-conversion instructions in ICC profiles, without having to re-invent the wheel for each application.

SPACES AND GAMUTS

To review Chapter 3, a *color space* describes the color model and characteristics of a given device. A *gamut* is the entire range of colors that can be reproduced within a given color space. Some devices, such as digital cameras, can produce colors that can't be accurately reproduced by other devices. Converting color from one space to another requires a method for handling colors that exist in the first space but not in the second.

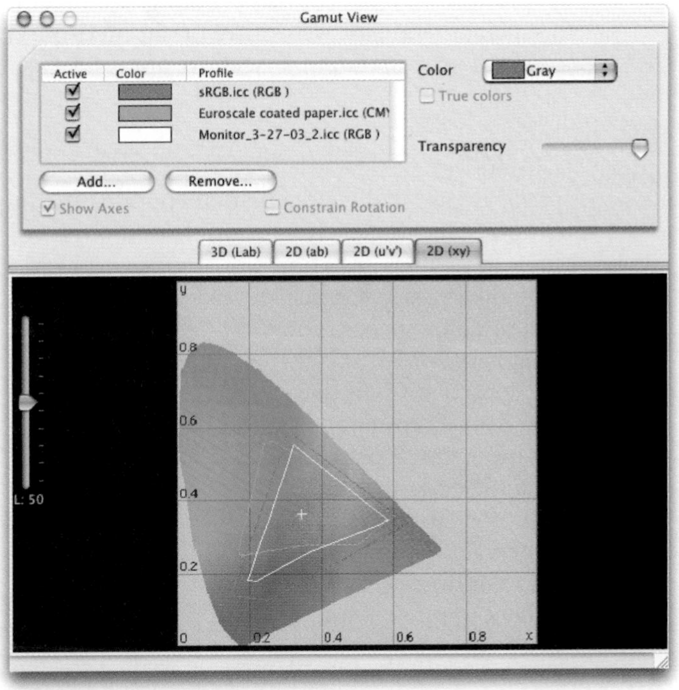

This diagram is a standard projection of the visible spectrum. The lines represent the gamuts of three color spaces: an RGB working space (sRGB), a CMYK working space (Euroscale Coated Paper), and a device-specific space (a profile made from a monitor). Colors outside the lines aren't reproducible in that space.

When we discuss color spaces, we can speak of three general categories:

- **Input Space**. Input (or *source*) space refers to the RGB color space of a particular image-capture device, such as a scanner or a digital camera. The color gamut of your monitor is also considered an input space, because you use the monitor to define and adjust colors in original artwork and acquired images. Input spaces are *device-dependent* because they represent the gamut of a particular device. For example, the color space of your scanner is unlike that of any other scanner; the differences may be small or large, but they exist even between two otherwise identical scanners.
- **Working Space**. This is a standardized color space used for portability of color. A working space is *device-independent* because its gamut is based on a theoretical gamut that can be easily reproduced on any computer system. It's not a requirement to use a working space when converting from an input space to an output space, but it's very useful when images are moved from one computer system to another.
- **Output Space**. Output (or *destination*) space refers to the RGB or CMYK model used by an output device such as an RGB photo printer, an inkjet printer, proofing equipment, or a printing process such as standard web-offset or sheetfed-offset lithography. Like input spaces, output spaces are always device-dependent.

PROFILES

A *profile* is essentially a recipe that contains the ingredients for reproducing a color as closely as possible in a given color space. The color recipes in profiles are known as "look-up tables" (LUTs), which are essentially cross-reference systems for finding matching color values in different color spaces. The *Color Management Module* (CMM) is the engine of a CMS that drives color conversions via the LUT numbers. Most CMMs are simple code that don't do much other than look up numbers and cross-reference them to another set of numbers.

> A test performed by Richard M. Adams II (published in *GATFWorld* magazine) concludes, "The choice of CMM makes far less difference than the choice of profiling software." Different profiling applications will generate slightly different profiles from the same set of measurement data. There's no standard defined for the techniques used to compute a profile, so everyone does it a little differently.

L*a*b*, as described in Chapter 3, is a theoretical color space that represents the visible spectrum. (Another theoretical space, XYZ, is sometimes used instead of L*a*b*.) These are device-independent color spaces that can represent any color. By moving device-dependent RGB and CMYK colors into L*a*b* or XYZ as an intermediary space, you can convert color from any one space to any other space, eliminating the need for specific LUTs for every possible combination of spaces, models, and device dependencies.

The mechanics of color-managed conversions are pretty simple. Color-managed conversions require two profiles: a source (or input) profile and a destination (or output) profile. Regardless of the specific input and output spaces in question, the same two-step process is followed for every pixel in the image:

1. The CMS looks up the color values of a pixel in the input-space profile to find a matching set of L*a*b* values.
2. The CMS looks up the L*a*b* values in the output-space profile to find the matching set of color values that will display the color of that pixel accurately in the output space.

Let's look at an example, where an image in the Adobe RGB (1998) working space (the input space) is converted for proper display on an Apple iBook monitor (the output space):

1. One pixel in the file has the value R:127 G:0 B:255.
2. Photoshop looks up these values in the Adobe RGB (1998) profile to find the matching L*a*b* color values L:43 a:78 b–92.
3. Photoshop looks for those L*a*b* values in the Apple iBook monitor profile, and finds the corresponding values R:155 G:0 B:255.
4. Photoshop sends those values to the iBook video controller for display on the screen, producing an accurate match to the original color on the monitor.

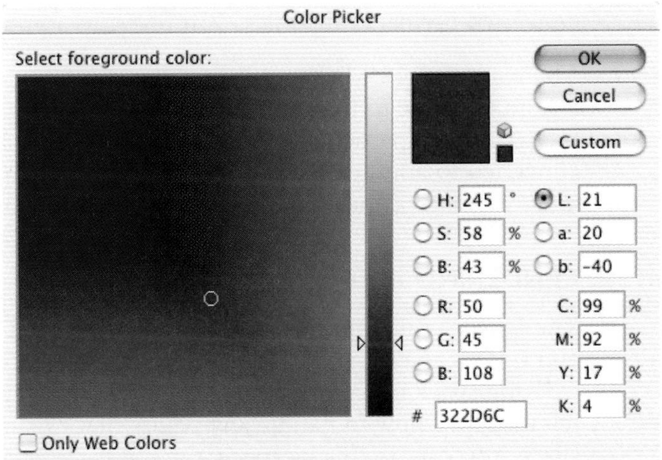

*To reproduce the L*a*b* color L:21 a:20 b:–40, a program like Photoshop can look in the monitor profile to learn the corresponding RGB values (R:50 G:45 B:108) needed to display that color (a dark blue) on the monitor being used.*

Once you get past the jargon, color management is easier to understand. One final example to help you follow the process used to change an RGB image to CMYK:

1. Photoshop sends the RGB values of a pixel to the CMM.
2. The CMM finds the RGB numbers in the look-up table of the image's RGB source profile.
3. The look-up table tells the CMM the L*a*b* or XYZ values of the color.
4. The CMM finds those L*a*b*/XYZ values in the look-up table of the selected CMYK destination profile and gets the CMYK values of the color.
5. The CMM sends those CMYK values back to Photoshop.
6. The process is repeated for all image pixels.

This type of conversion happens automatically, behind the scenes. The color values in the image aren't changed; they're simply used to calculate matching color values for display on the monitor.

Explicitly converting an image from one space to another works the same way — the color-management system takes input or working-space color data to L*a*b*, then to an output or another working space. The changes in the image data can be permanent, depending on how the conversion is done.

If you print an RGB image to a CMYK printer and enable color management for printing, then your application converts the RGB data to the printer's CMYK space "on the fly" — the original image will remain untouched. But if you change the color mode in an image-editing application such as Photoshop, the image data in the file is converted permanently unless you revert to a previously saved version.

There are many CMYK profiles — every different printer and press has a gamut unique to that individual device. If an image is permanently converted to a particular output space, it cannot later be easily converted to another. It's much easier and more accurate to separate an RGB image as needed for specific CMYK printing conditions.

RENDERING INTENTS

The L*a*b* color space has the largest gamut, RGB the next largest, and CMYK the smallest. If you need to convert an image from an RGB working space to a more limited CMYK output space, you first need to tell the CMS how to handle any colors that exist outside the CMYK space. You can do this by specifying the *rendering intent* of the image when starting a conversion.

An intent is one of four special LUTs that are part of an ICC profile, used by an application's CMS to manage the color-conversion process.

You can *usually* choose from four different rendering intents, each of which defines a unique conversion method to accommodate various types of images. (Some programs don't let you choose an intent; they default to the perceptual option.)

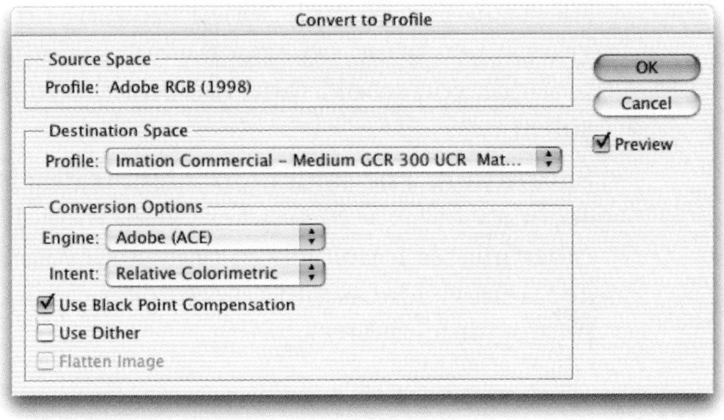

Choose a rendering intent in Photoshop's Conversion Options in the Convert to Profile dialog box.

- **Perceptual**. The perceptual intent uses gamut compression, where all colors in the image are compressed based on human color perception; overall saturation is decreased slightly, and luminance can change, but the relationship between all colors is preserved, so the image looks pretty much the same perceptually as it did before.

  Gamut compression is a disadvantage if you start with an image that's already in the gamut of the destination profile. A CMS isn't smart enough to know that an image is in-gamut, so gamut compression occurs with this intent whether you need it or not.

- **Relative Colorimetric**. The relative colorimetric intent uses gamut clipping. Out-of-gamut colors in the source image are converted to their closest available matches in the destination gamut; the clipped colors have reduced saturation and might be a little lighter, but the hues are preserved. In-gamut colors are unchanged.

  The downside of this intent is that different out-of-gamut colors can be converted to the same in-gamut color, leading to loss of detail or *posterization* in clipped areas. Images with bright detail, for example, could be damaged by using this intent.

> RGB working-space profiles only contain one rendering intent — relative colorimetric — but most other profiles generally contain all four.

Deciding whether to use the perceptual or relative colorimetric intent depends on the type of image. Try both, and see which one you like better. There is no hard-and-fast rule about picking rendering intents other than taking them for a test drive.

- **Absolute Colorimetric**. The absolute colorimetric intent is the same as the relative colorimetric intent, except it doesn't remap media white points across profiles. Converted images simulate the white point of the destination profile, which is useful when proofing on media with a different white point than the final substrate. For example, when proofing images intended for dull, grayish newsprint on bright-white inkjet media or on your monitor, you would want the proof to reflect the color of the final substrate.
- **Saturation**. The saturation intent is designed to sacrifice color accuracy in favor of apparent saturation. It's useful for charts and other images for which color accuracy isn't as important as apparent vividness and colorfulness. This is not a good option for photographic images.

Creating Profiles

To fully take advantage of the capabilities of color management, you must define a color profile for every device in your workflow. You can either create your own profiles, or use the "canned" profiles included with many devices and applications. Creating high-quality profiles requires a serious commitment in time and money. Each device (including every monitor, printer, proofer, scanner, printing press, digital camera, film recorder, video-frame grabber, and any other machine in your facility) must be profiled with specialized software and often with specialized equipment.

You'll need to spend some money to create input (scanner, camera) and output (printer) profiles. It's cheaper to make input profiles; the software to do this typically costs a few hundred dollars. To make output profiles, you need a specialized instrument called a "spectrophotometer," which measures the wavelengths of light reflected back to it from a surface — a printed page, a paint swatch, or even a flower petal — to measure the reproduction characteristics of a printer, press, proofer, or other device. A spectrophotometer and good-quality profiling software can cost $1,500 or more.

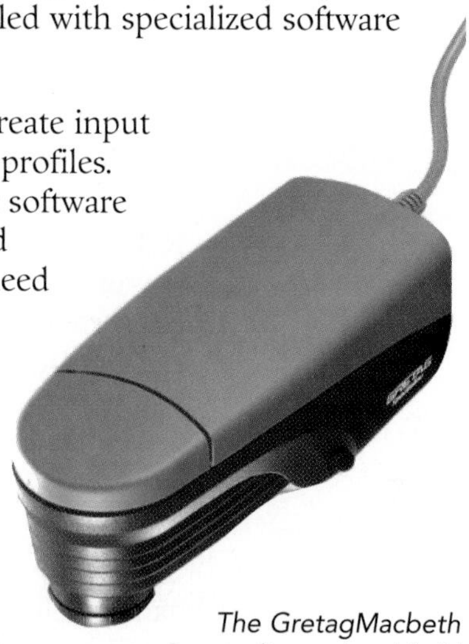

The GretagMacbeth Spectrolino, a hand-held spectrophotometer.

MONITOR PROFILES

The one profile that is easy and inexpensive to create is a monitor profile; you can easily create a monitor profile using the Adobe Gamma utility (installed automatically on Windows computers with most Adobe applications) or the Apple Monitor Calibrator utility.

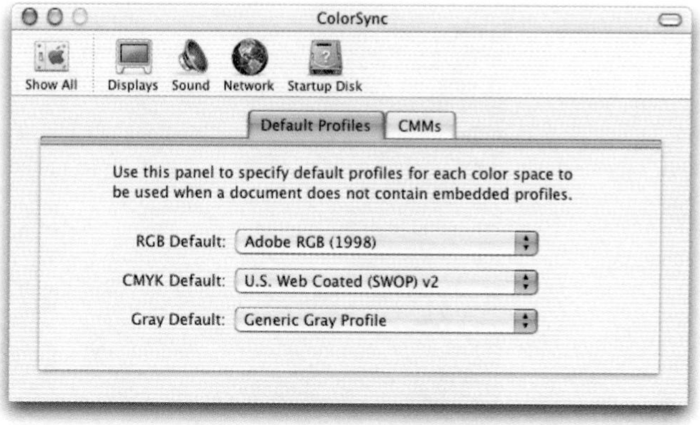

Apple's Display Calibrator Assistant (OS X).

When using either software-calibration utility, we recommend using the following settings:

- Gamma 2.2 (PC) or 1.8 (Macintosh).
- White point adjusted to D65/6500K for Web images, D50/5000K for print images.

COLORSYNC PREFERENCES

After creating a monitor profile, you can use the ColorSync preferences in the Control Panels (Mac OS 9) or System Preferences (Mac OS X) to set default profiles for new documents and to set desired working spaces. Very little software, however, actually looks at your ColorSync settings. It's up to software developers to take advantage of this operating-system feature; it's possible that future applications will make use of this information. You can force Photoshop and other Adobe applications to use these ColorSync settings by choosing "ColorSync" in the working-space profile menus. Windows has no analogous profile setup preference.

SCANNER PROFILES

To profile a scanner, you need a *target* — a carefully manufactured photographic print or slide that has been measured by the manufacturer with a spectrophotometer. These targets are available on a variety of photographic films and papers, all of which have slightly different reproduction characteristics. You can be very specific with input profiles, creating different ones for different types of media. Some people create separate profiles for different types of film and paper.

Most input targets are variations of the IT8.7/2 target, shown below. They differ in the media on which they are imaged, and in the layout of the patches. For example, Kodak includes a photo of a woman, while Agfa and Fuji use additional color patches in the same area.

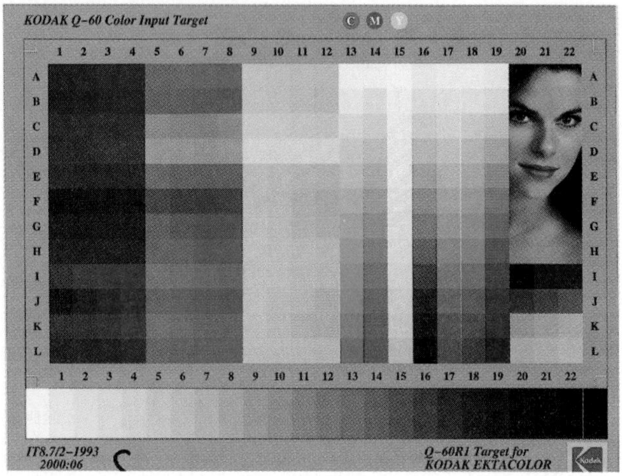

The Kodak Q-60 photographic scanner target.
Note the date and batch number in the lower-left corner.

There are no targets for color-negative films. First, you don't want to reproduce the orange mask used in negative film. In addition, variations in exposure and processing make negative film impractical to profile. There is no way to guarantee using the same film, processing chemistry, temperature, time, exposures, and so forth *all the time*.

Most quality desktop scanners ship with an IT8 target in one or more media (paper as well as transparency). Many manufacturers also include profiles for their devices.

The other problem with profiling negatives is that you can't be sure what the original scene looked like unless you photographed it yourself. If someone gives you negatives to scan, you have no point of reference from the original scene. It would be very difficult to produce a reference negative target of, for example, the IT8.7/2; the colors hidden in a negative are subjective and can't be measured and quantified, unlike the color patches of a printed target or one made from color reversal (slide) film.

To use the target to create a profile for your scanner, you first scan the target to a TIFF file, then use your profiling software to calculate a profile using the scan of the target and the target's color-data file.

Make sure the data file you use with the profiling software matches the target's production date and batch code. Profiling software that comes with a target should include the data file for that target. The details may differ, but for most profiling software, you align a grid to the scanned target's color patches.

> It's very important when scanning a target to turn off all of the automatic adjustment settings in your scanner software. Otherwise you won't get an accurate representation of its ability to capture image data.

You'll usually need to align and resize a grid like this to a scan of an IT8.7/2 target prior to creating a scanner profile.

CAMERA PROFILES

Profiling digital cameras is often not worth the effort unless you are shooting in a studio with consistent lighting, exposure, and focal-length settings. Unlike a scanner, a digital camera captures images under an infinite number of lighting conditions, shutter speeds, f-stops, simulated ISO film speed, and more variables.

Digital cameras have been designed to perform varying levels of color management internally. Nikon's high-end D1x cameras, for example, perform a color-managed conversion of raw sensor data to the Adobe RGB working space based on a specified chosen white-point setting.

Assuming the shot is made correctly, this is a safe way to get what you expect from the camera. Some cameras simply tag image data with the sRGB working space without doing any kind of conversion, which is better than nothing.

There are a few profiling software packages that claim to profile digital cameras, but they are expensive. The special targets are expensive too — they need to be much larger than scanner targets, and they're made of painted patches instead of photographic paper, which is not a suitable medium for camera profiling because you can't effectively shoot a photo of a photo.

PRINTER PROFILES

To profile a printer or other output media, you print another type of target —usually a TIFF or EPS file — on the device to be profiled. To get an accurate representation of the device's color-reproduction range, you need to turn off any type of automatic adjustments and enhancements in the printer's driver setup. Once the target is printed, you measure each patch of color with a spectrophotometer, then save the measurement data to a file. Your profiling software uses that data along with the known color values in the target to generate a profile of the device's output characteristics. For each measured color patch in the target, the software looks at the L*a*b* color values in the target's data file and correlates these to the original RGB or CMYK color values in the printed target.

For example, a solid block defined as C:70 M:20 Y:70 K:0 is printed, then measured with a spectrophotometer. The spectrophotometer returns the value L:56 a:–27 b:17. A profile made for that printer contains data that basically tells a program:

> if you print
>
> > 70, 20, 70, 0,
>
> then the CMYK color translates to L*a*b*
>
> > 56, –27, 17.

This simple correlation enables programs such as Photoshop to predict what a given color mix in RGB or CMYK will look like both on-screen and in print; it also provides an easy way to convert, using L*a*b* (or XYZ) as an intermediary, between different color spaces.

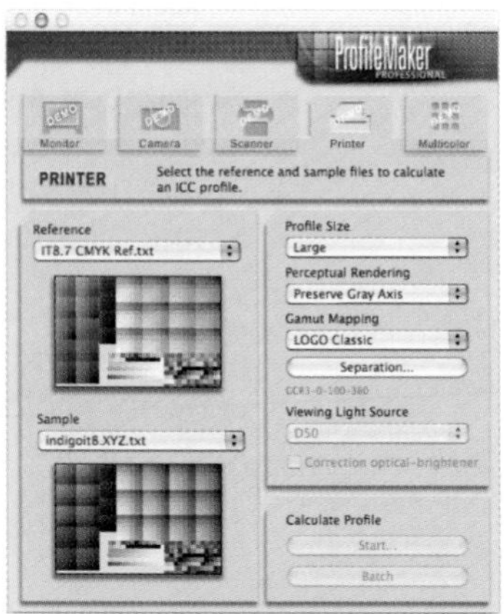

Setting the target reference and measured target-color data prior to profile creation.

Printed targets are typically measured with some type of automated mechanism to relieve you of having to manually measure and record the values for thousands of little squares.

The GretagMacbeth SpectroScan x/y table automatically measures each patch on a printed target. Note the Spectrolino attached to the scanning mechanism

There are a few standard printer targets, but most profiling software packages use proprietary targets, and few packages can make use of targets from other packages. If it's important to use a single target with different profiling packages, use the IT8.7/3 or ECI printer targets, which are included with most profiling software packages.

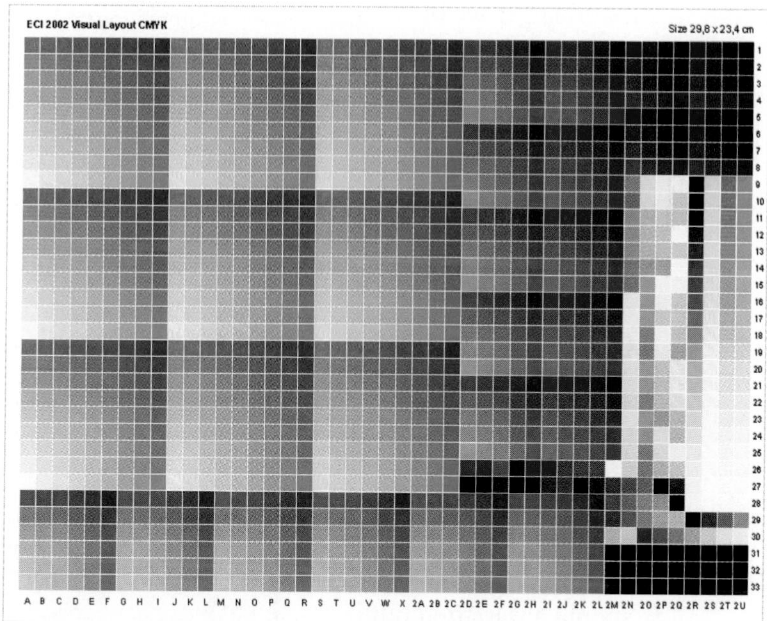

The new ECI 2002 CMYK printer/press target.

USING PROFILES

Once the appropriate profiles are defined, they can be assigned to images in several different ways. A profile can be embedded within an image and interpreted by an application for display and printing purposes. Alternatively, profiles can be stored on disk, assigned to images as needed, and read from disk by applications for screen display of untagged images. Profiles need to be copied to the following locations for the operating system and applications to use them:

Mac OS X
Macintosh HD>Library>ColorSync>Profiles, or
User Folder>Library>ColorSync>Profiles

Mac OS 9
Macintosh HD>System Folder>ColorSync

Windows XP/2000
Windows>System32>Spool>Drivers>Color

Windows 98/ME
Windows>System>Color

If an image is in an RGB space, you should always embed the correct profile — whether it is a working space or a device space — when saving the file. This is the default behavior for Photoshop and most other color-managed applications. If an image lacks an embedded profile, you usually can't tell which RGB space was used without a great deal of trial and error. For CMYK images, embedding a profile enables more accurate screen previews and proofing.

> You can only embed a profile that matches the image color model. In other words, you can't embed a CMYK profile into an RGB image, and you can't embed an RGB profile into a CMYK image.

Color Management in Adobe Applications

The primary benefit of using a color-managed system is that it provides very accurate previews of imported color images, color and gradient swatches, and other types of artwork.

The primary drawback of working in a color-managed environment is that few service providers and printers understand how to use ICC color management. You should always find out if your printer accepts color-managed jobs. If not, you should either find a different printer who *can* work with color-managed files, or avoid using color-

> Other applications (QuarkXPress, CorelDRAW, Macromedia FreeHand, and others) follow the same principles as Adobe when configuring their color-management options, although the nomenclature is often different.

management options to generate your output. (You can still use color management to display images and colors accurately, you just need to turn it off before submitting the final job to the printer to prevent any inadvertent color conversions.)

Adobe's color-management system — used in Photoshop, Illustrator, and InDesign — includes several predefined settings appropriate for a variety of workflows. For on-screen display, you can choose the Web option; for printed material, you can choose the appropriate prepress setup. If you prefer to create your own customized settings, you need to define the working spaces, color-management policies, and conversion options. You can import and export color-management settings between most Adobe applications.

> Note that Adobe PageMaker does not use the same color-management system as other Adobe applications, because PageMaker is essentially an Aldus product that Adobe acquired some time ago. The color management in PageMaker is flawed and should not be used.

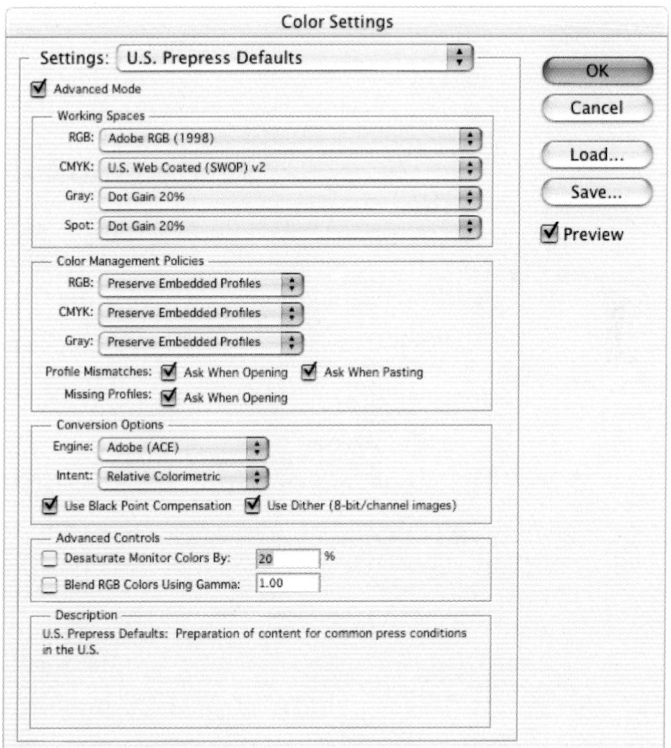

The U.S. Prepress Default color-management settings in Photoshop 7.

The RGB working-space menu lists all RGB profiles installed on your computer. The first four are working spaces, which are installed when you first install the software.

- Adobe RGB (1998) working space, which we recommend, is the default for the U.S. Prepress setting.
- The Apple RGB option approximates the behavior of the original Apple 13-in. color monitor and should not be used.
- ColorMatch RGB is a smaller-gamut working space intended to match the display of the outdated Radius PressMatch monitor.
- sRGB is a small-gamut RGB space intended for Web graphics.

This menu also lists the monitor profiles that you can create with various utilities, and, for Macintosh users, the RGB profile identified as the RGB default in the ColorSync settings. Any other RGB profiles listed in this pop-up menu are probably device profiles that should not be used as a working space.

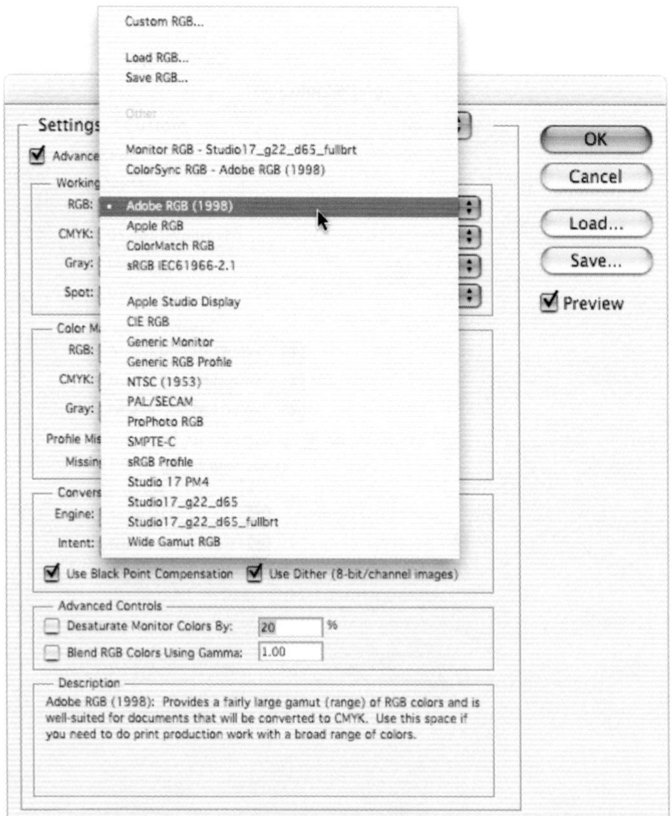

The four standard RGB working spaces are displayed at the top of the menu, followed by your current monitor profile, then the default RGB document profile that you can define in the ColorSync workflow setup (Macintosh only). Device-specific RGB profiles are displayed last.

Your choice in the CMYK working-space menu depends on the kind of printing you plan to do. For most commercial printing, you should choose U.S. Sheetfed Coated or U.S. Web Coated (SWOP). Other options in this list may be custom CMYK profiles that you have created and installed on your computer. Because CMYK is by nature device-dependent, it is acceptable to set this menu to a specific device profile.

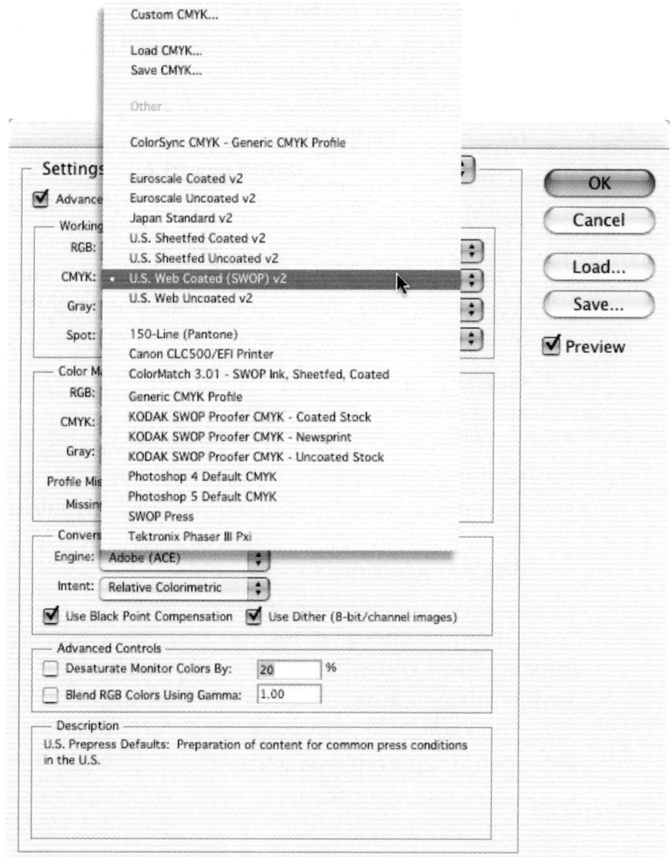

Similar to the RGB pop-up menu, the CMYK working-space menu lists Adobe-installed CMYK working-space profiles first. The ones following these are custom or device-specific profiles that may be used as a working space.

COLOR-MANAGEMENT POLICIES

You will often receive files created by people who used different working spaces, or no color management at all. You can tell Photoshop and other Adobe applications how to handle the color management of such imported images by setting up color-management *policies*, which are nothing more than simple rules.

In Photoshop's Color Settings dialog box, you can define separate policies for RGB and CMYK images.

- **Off**. This option simply means that policies are off; it does not turn color management off, except for new files and for images that use a working space that matches your current working space. For each working space, color values in swatches, imported images, and imported graphics are used without adjustment for your display. Basically, it means that any embedded profiles are used for display and saved with the file; you just aren't made aware of their existence.
- **Preserve Embedded Profiles**. This option uses any embedded profiles in the document even if they don't match your current working spaces. The software tries to match color appearance for RGB images, and uses the numeric values in CMYK images for screen display. Unless you know that the embedded profiles are wrong for your needs, you should typically choose this setting. You can always convert to another space later.
- **Convert to Working Space**. If the imported document's working space doesn't match your current working space, this option converts color data to the current working space. This can be useful if you need to incorporate someone else's work into your own color-managed workflow, but it shouldn't be used for CMYK files, which are already in a device-dependent color space and don't convert nicely to another.

You can choose to have the software alert you when a profile mismatch occurs. Mismatches can occur when you open documents, or when you paste objects in from other applications. If you don't want to be notified about mismatches, deselect the check boxes.

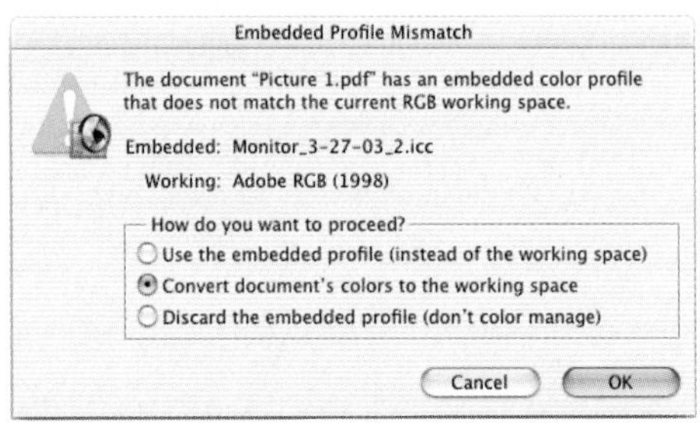

Profile mismatch for an RGB image.

A fourth policy option, Missing Profiles, directs the software to alert you when it opens a document with a missing profile. In the warning dialog box that appears, you can assign the current working space or another profile to the document.

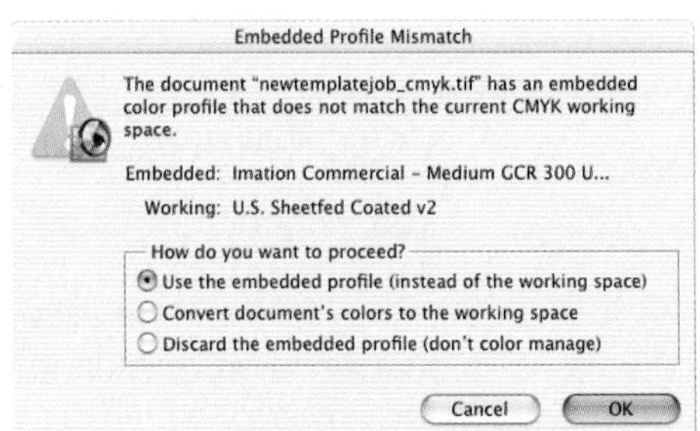

Profile mismatch for a CMYK image. Generally you want to use the embedded profile, or discard it.

If you choose Leave As Is, the document is temporarily color-managed for display, but color-management information is not saved when you close it. This is useful when you exchange documents with others who aren't using color management.

When opening images with missing profiles, Photoshop and other Adobe applications will still use the working spaces specified in the Color Settings control panel to define the display colors for the image; no profiles will be embedded in the image file.

Typically it's safe to not color-manage CMYK images that lack embedded profiles. (Of course, this assumes that the images were correctly converted to CMYK. Sometimes this isn't the case, but there's not much you can do to fix a bad separation.) If you know which CMYK profile was used to separate an image that lacks a profile, you can assign that profile for the best on-screen preview. As a last resort you can convert the image to L*a*b* or RGB, then convert it back to CMYK using your preferred CMYK profile.

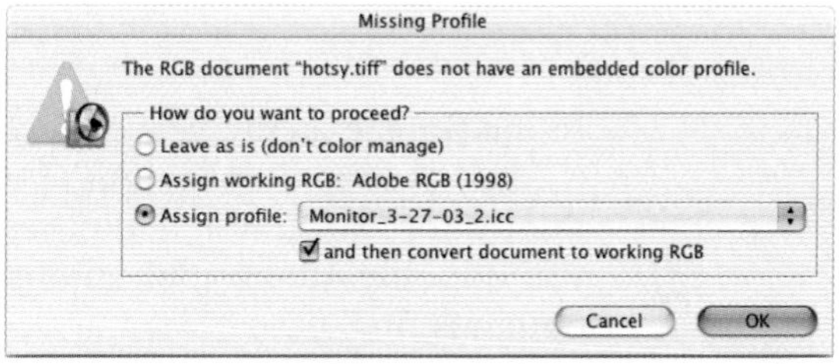

Warning of a missing RGB profile. Here, a monitor profile is the input space (standard for screen shots); it's being converted to the chosen working space.

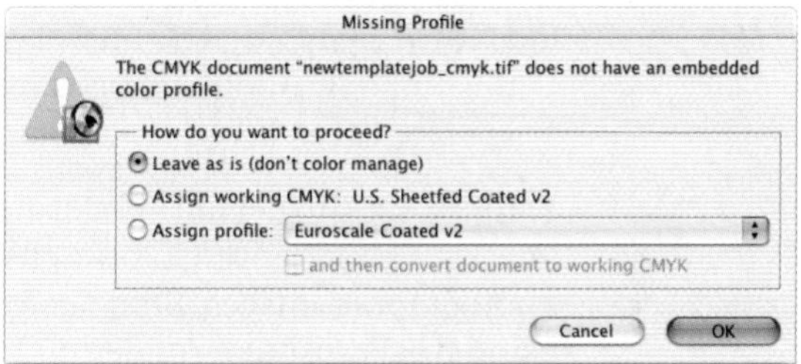

Warning of a missing CMYK profile. Here, we tell Photoshop not to color-manage the image.

Converting CMYK data from one space to another isn't recommended; it's best to keep original images in an RGB working space, and to convert to CMYK spaces as needed. You can get away with converting a large-gamut CMYK image prepared for sheetfed-offset printing to a lower-gamut CMYK space such as that needed for newspaper printing. Going the other way, however, results in muddy, low-contrast images because you can't resurrect data lost in a large-to-small gamut conversion.

COLOR-CONVERSION OPTIONS

Other options appear when you check Advanced Mode in Photoshop's Color Settings dialog box. These same options are also available when using the Photoshop Convert to Profile command.

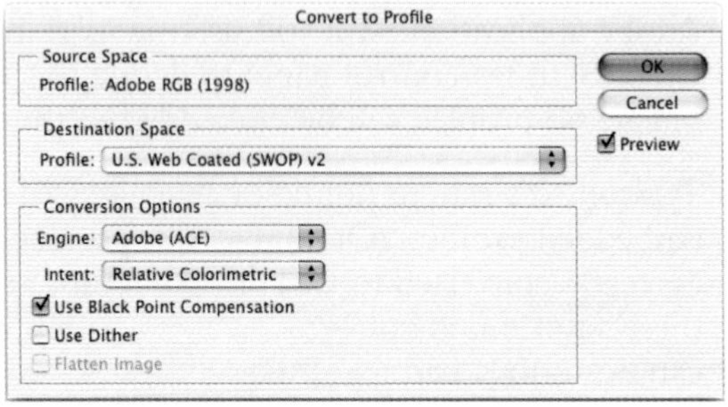

In the Engine menu, you can select a Color Management Module (CMM). Adobe Color Engine (ACE), which is built into InDesign, Photoshop, Illustrator, and other Adobe applications, is the default. If you use only Adobe applications in a color-managed workflow, this option is fine.

In general, ACE is the most current, reliable color-management conversion engine. If you perform color-space conversions with non-Adobe applications that let you choose a CMM, you should choose the CMM matching the one used in those other applications. Unfortunately, Adobe embeds its CMM within its software, so it's not a separate file you can install and use with other applications.

You can set the default rendering intent used to convert and display images. The Relative Colorimetric option typically works best for photographic images. Some color-management experts recommend using the Perceptual rendering intent. Try both to determine which works best for your image. Most images convert best with the Relative Colorimetric intent, but some with very bright, saturated colors may look better using the Perceptual intent.

The Black Point Compensation option should be turned on in most cases. This feature matches the black point of an image (the darkest color in an image) when it is converted from one color model to another, such as from RGB to CMYK. Without it, blacks and dark grays in an image can become washed out and weak.

When converting an image from one RGB space to another, this option can have the opposite effect. Experimentation is the best way to determine whether this option should be on or off. The Preview check box in this and other Photoshop dialog boxes is very useful.

The Dither option is used to simulate a source color in the destination gamut if the source color doesn't exist in the destination. You can only select the Flatten Image option when a Photoshop file contains layers.

Color Management in QuarkXPress

QuarkCMS is the color-management system built into QuarkXPress. It is included with the application as an XTension, and must be active to function within the software. QuarkCMS is the interface through which you control the CMM in the Quark environment. The color-management settings are accessed in the application preferences.

When you first access the Color Management Preferences dialog box, you have to select the Color Management Active check box to define the settings. You can choose Destination Profiles for the monitor, composite printer, and separation printer you are using; and Source Profiles for RGB, CMYK, and Hexachrome colors and images.

QuarkXPress offers the same rendering intents available in Adobe applications: Perceptual, Relative Colorimetric, Saturation, and Absolute Colorimetric.

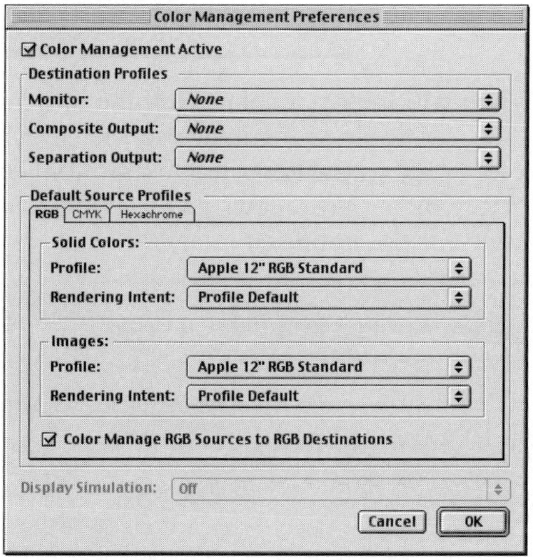

The Color Manage RGB Sources to RGB Destinations check box allows you to color-manage files between different RGB color spaces. The biggest problem of color shift occurs when moving between different color spaces (e.g., RGB to CMYK). Because there is some variation, however, between the output of different monitors and RGB printers, you may want to select this option.

After you have defined the destination profiles in the Monitor, Composite Output, and Separation Output menus, the Display Simulation menu becomes available, and enables you to approximate — on your monitor — the color space of

> QuarkXPress color management only applies to placed images. It does not affect CMYK builds or spot colors in the application's Colors palette.

your intended output device. If this option is turned off, you will not see any color difference on your monitor.

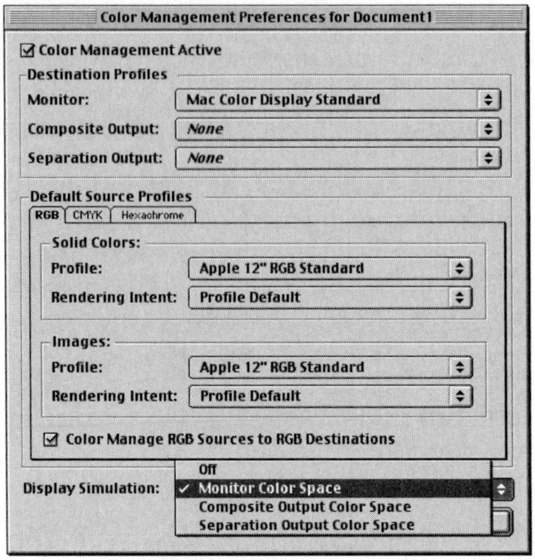

When you import a color TIFF file into a Quark layout, you can attach a source profile to the image so the CMM correctly translates the color space to the appropriate monitor. The bottom half of the Get Picture dialog box allows you to choose the profile and rendering intent for the imported image.

Because RGB monitors simply do not reproduce the same gamut as CMYK printers, the accuracy of color-display simulation is questionable. Color management is an inexact science. For a truly color-managed workflow to exist, the devices — input and output — used in the workflow need to be calibrated regularly and profiled. Some experts recommend calibration as often as every week; others believe that monthly calibration is adequate. If your input and output devices are not calibrated, color management is only a theory.

So, why use a color-management system?

If you are operating a true color-managed workflow — all devices calibrated regularly and ICC profiles for every device installed — color management can help you maintain consistent color from the initial scan to the printed page. QuarkCMS allows you to integrate a Quark document into a fully color-managed workflow.

If you have not properly calibrated your equipment or do not have the appropriate ICC profiles, QuarkCMS can still help to approximate the final output on your monitor. Keep in mind, however, that what you see is not necessarily what you will get.

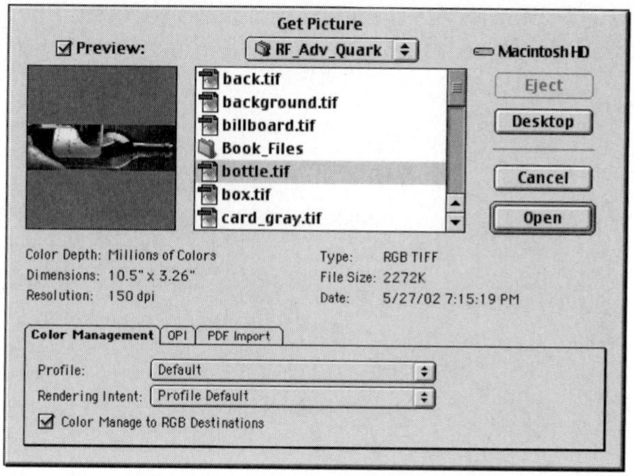

If you import an image with an embedded profile into QuarkXPress, the Profile menu defaults to Embedded. There is, however, no way to determine exactly *which* profile is embedded. You can replace the embedded profile by choosing another profile from the Profile menu.

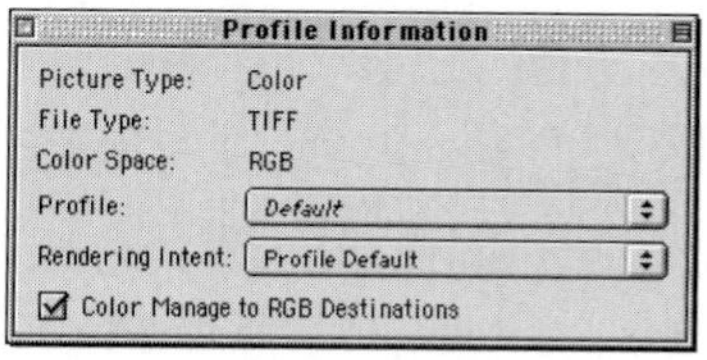

You can also change the profile of an image that is already placed. The Profile Information dialog box shows the picture type, file type, and color space of the image selected in the document window. The Profile and Rendering Intent menus can be changed to any other existing profiles.

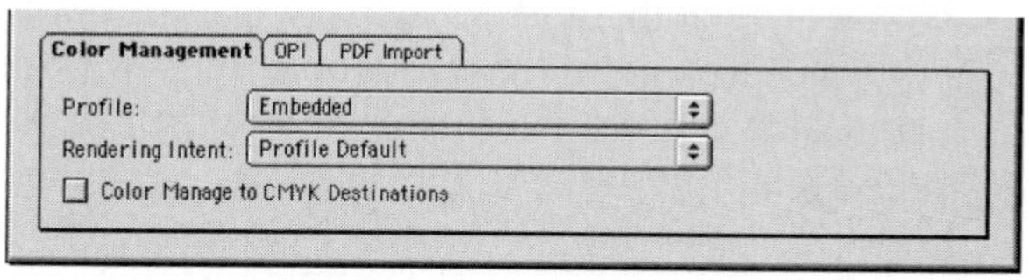

Color Management for Electronic Media

Adobe Acrobat supports color management for screen viewing, but chances are good that most people have never set up their monitors to allow this. Although some Web browsers support ICC color management, and the JPEG image format widely used for Web graphics supports embedded ICC profiles, few Web surfers have ever calibrated their monitors, much less created profiles for them.

Currently, the only browsers to support embedded image profiles are Microsoft Internet Explorer for Mac OS 9 and X, and OmniWeb 4.5 for Mac OS X.

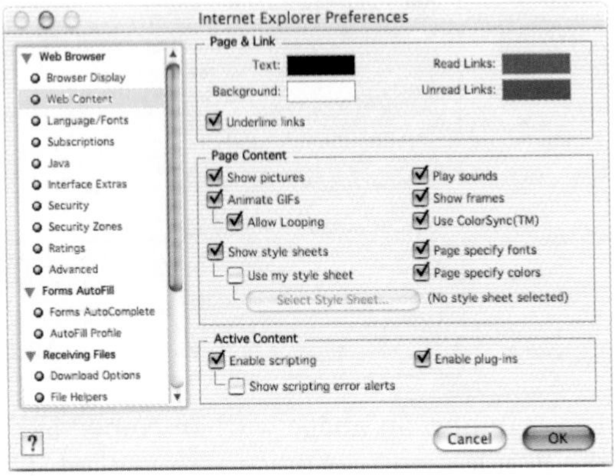

ColorSync color matching can be enabled in the Internet Explorer preferences with the Use ColorSync check box.

The Windows version of Internet Explorer does not directly support embedded image profiles; as nearly all other Web browsers do, it assumes that Web images are in the sRGB color space. Color management can be important in e-commerce, especially for products such as clothing for which color is a critical attribute, but the technology is seldom used even there. Embedded RGB profiles are very small (typically less than 4 Kb), though, so embedding them into JPEG images used for Web pages won't cause any undue stress for most Web users.

Conclusion

Color management allows you to accurately preview printed colors on your monitor, as well as provide some assurance that the colors printed on a proof will match the output from a commercial printing press. It is important to have realistic expectations of color management. To work properly, color management requires careful calibration for all equipment in your workflow. Color management doesn't work if you don't have accurate device profiles, it can't cause RGB devices to produce CMYK color, and it can't fix bad images. Color management *can*, however, provide consistency and predictability to a process that otherwise rarely has either.

CHAPTER 7

Color Correction

In a perfect world, all photographs would be crisp and clear, and all scans would be optimally balanced with beautiful, accurate color. In the real world, however, digital images come from a variety of sources, and many are far from perfect. To reproduce an image, regardless of the condition of the original source file, you must be able to effectively use the variety of image-adjustment tools.

The goal of color correction is to produce the best possible image for reproduction in a specific output medium, whether digital or printed. There are many reasons why images need to be corrected — including poor contrast, overly strong or weak saturation, and visible color casts. Although the actual process of correcting an image should be based on numbers, evaluating the need for correction can be far more subjective:

- **Memory Colors.** Memory colors — the colors that our memories tell us objects should be — play an important part in how we perceive the content of an image. Many thousands of marketing research dollars have been spent to determine that people expect lemons to be yellow, grass to be green, and the sky to be blue. Color correction, then, plays an important role in product marketing. Much of the work we do as designers will enhance the appearance of a product — manipulating color balance, saturation, and brightness to make a product more appealing.
- **Product Matching.** Color correction is an extremely important aspect of product marketing. In addition to faithful reproduction of memory colors, many products are inherently linked to the appearance of their packaging. Coca-Cola, for example, has a specifically formulated and copyrighted red ink that is found on every can, bottle, and box used to package its products. Although few people will need to specify Coca-Cola Red in an image, the concept of accurately reproducing product colors is very important in the color-correction process.
- **Editorial Correction.** When you work with clients, you hear interesting directions such as, "I want that red sweater to pop off the page," or "Make that orange juicier!" Despite the best efforts of software developers, we simply don't

have "Pop" or "Juicy" filters to apply to our work. We do, however, have a series of powerful tools that can be used to enhance images, making it possible to manipulate the appearance of images to meet most (though never all) client demands.

- **Accuracy vs. Artist's Intent.** Professional photographers — especially those who photograph human models — spend a great deal of time creating moods. They use filters, special lighting, and other techniques to create the perfect photo for a specific need. These techniques often include an intentional color cast to set a mood — red to add warmth, or blue to create a clean, cool feeling. If you correct this type of image to create "accurate" neutrals (in other words, remove the color cast), you effectively destroy the artist's original intent. Ultimately, it is the client who decides what and how much correction you should perform. In many cases, you will probably correct some of the cast, but not all.

Environmental Considerations

Before you begin to correct color, remember that your monitor is an RGB device. If you are correcting for print, you are preparing images that will be output as CMYK. You have learned — and it bears repeating — that there are inherent differences between the color displayed on your monitor and the color printed on a page.

Chapter 6 discussed color-management techniques, which are vital to an accurate color-reproduction process. Ideally, every device in your workflow should be profiled and calibrated. But even without color management in place, you can still produce quality color reproductions if you keep this thought firmly in the front of your mind — base color corrections on numbers rather than only what you see on your screen.

> Designers often make subjective color decisions, by visually inspecting the appearance of images on their screen. Most imaging gurus, however, maintain that correcting "by the numbers" is the best approach.

Having said that, most people (including us) still correct color by looking at the colors on the monitor. Given this insistence on subjective decision-making, it's important to make sure you're seeing the colors as accurately as possible. In addition to using color-management techniques to calibrate your monitor, you should also consider how environmental factors can affect how color appears on your monitor. Keep in mind when you set up your office to perform color corrections:

- The light in your office or workspace can affect what you see on the screen. Any room with windows should have blinds or some other covering because natural light is inconsistent. Most professionals prefer to work in the dark when correcting color.

- The walls in your workspace should be a neutral color, preferably a neutral gray. Surround color (such as purple walls) can affect the color you see on your monitor.
- Wear neutral-color clothing. Like purple walls, a bright red shirt can reflect onto a monitor and affect the color you see on the screen. If you insist on wearing bright clothes, invest in a gray artist's smock to wear while correcting color.
- Set your monitor to 5000K if you're correcting for print, 6500K if you're correcting for the Web.

Many professional designers also have a small 5000K viewing booth on their desktops so they can quickly compare color to the original.

Applying Color Theory

The relationship between additive and subtractive primary colors is the foundation of basic color correction. To review from Chapter 3:

- Combining any two additive primary colors (red, green, and blue) results in one of the subtractive primaries (cyan, magenta, and yellow). This relationship means that the subtractive primaries are also the additive secondaries.
- Conversely (using the subtractive color model), combining any two subtractive primaries results in one of the additive primaries. This relationship means that the additive primaries are also the subtractive secondaries.
- A *color complement* is the color located directly opposite on the color wheel. For example, green is the complement of magenta because green is the one color in the RGB triangle that is not included when making pure magenta. Adding the complement of a color neutralizes its brilliance, and causes the color to become grayish (less saturated).

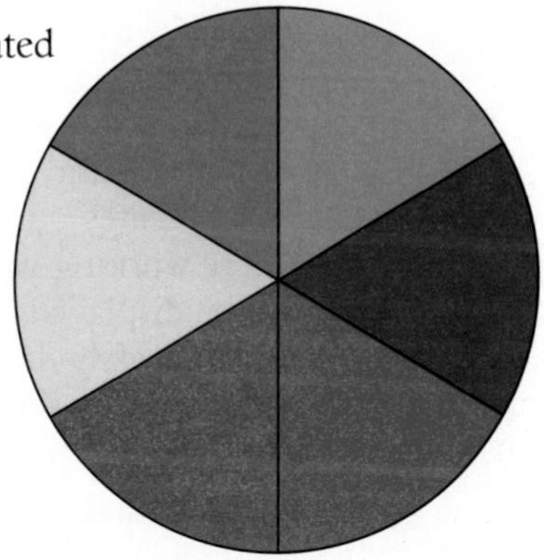

If you want to add a specific color to an image, you have three options:

- Add the color.
- Add equal parts of the color's component colors.
- Remove some of the color's complement.

For example, to add red to an image, you could add red, add yellow and magenta, or remove cyan.

Conversely, this means that to remove a color from an image, you can:

- Remove the color itself.
- Remove equal parts of the color's components.
- Add the color's complement.

To remove cyan from an image, for example, you could remove cyan, remove blue and green, or add red.

Although it seems easiest to add or subtract the color in question, better results might be achieved by adding one color and subtracting another. For example, if an image needs less blue, simply removing cyan could cause reds to appear pink or cyan to appear green. Adding magenta and yellow to balance the existing cyan could create a better result than simply removing cyan. The best results, however, are achieved by using a combination of these two techniques — removing some cyan, *and* adding some magenta and yellow.

> An important point to remember is that any color correction requires compromise. If you add or remove a color to correct a certain area, you also affect other areas of the image.

GRAY BALANCE

Another concept explained by color theory — creating neutral gray — is also fundamental to effective color correction. The RGB model uses light to create color, so equal parts of red, green, and blue combine to create neutral shades of gray equal to the amount of each component — R:0 G:0 B:0 creates pure black, and R:255 G:255 B:255 creates pure white. If you're working with images that will be displayed electronically, you can safely define pure black and white "by the numbers" using these values.

> Understanding the concept of neutral gray is fundamental to effective color correction. Many color problems can be at least partially (if not entirely) corrected by correcting the *gray balance*, or the component elements of neutral grays within an image.

The CMYK model uses pigments to create color, so equal parts of cyan, magenta, and yellow inks combine — in theory — to create neutral shades of gray that are equal to the percentage of each component. For example, 40% cyan, 40% magenta, and 40% yellow should combine to produce a 40% gray shade. In theory, solid black should be created by C:100 M:100 Y:100 K:0; white would be 0% of all the inks.

In practice, however, the pigments used to create printing inks are impure, each containing some of the light-filtering quality of the other primary inks. This is called "hue error" or "hue contamination."

The left block, which appears more brown than gray, is comprised of equal parts cyan, magenta, and yellow. The right block, composed of 50% cyan, 40% magenta, and 40% yellow, appears to be a properly neutral gray.

Because of this impurity, combining equal amounts of cyan, magenta, and yellow inks yields a reddish-brown rather than a neutral gray. To correct for hue contamination, a 5:4:4 ratio of cyan, magenta, and yellow inks should be applied. The increased percentage of cyan achieves a proper visual gray balance, resulting in neutrals that appear truly neutral instead of reddish.

UNDERSTANDING CHANNELS

Each color component of an image is called a "channel." Images in RGB color space have three color channels — the red channel, the green channel, and the blue channel. CMYK images have four channels — the cyan channel, the magenta channel, the yellow channel, and the black channel.

The concept of color channels can become confusing when you realize that each "color" channel actually contains only grayscale information. The grayscale representation within a specific channel defines the intensity of that primary color throughout the image.

When you correct color, you can apply changes to all channels simultaneously, or to individual channels. The ability to modify individual channels is extremely useful, for example, when correcting color cast.

All channels.

Each color channel defines the intensity of a single primary color throughout an image.

Cyan channel.

Magenta channel.

Yellow channel.

Black channel.

Which Mode?

Different designers have their own opinions about whether to correct in RGB or CMYK mode. In general, it is more efficient to convert to the output color mode, then correct the image. If your output goal is a digital medium (Internet, CD-ROM, or otherwise), there is little reason to convert to CMYK for correction. In this case, correcting in RGB makes sense.

When working on files that will be printed, however, there are other issues to consider. Most importantly, when an image is converted to CMYK for printing, some color shift occurs to compress RGB colors into the smaller CMYK gamut. If you correct an image in RGB mode, then convert it to CMYK, you might have to apply additional correction once the colors have shifted.

Many people (especially those who understand the basics of commercial color printing) find it easier to correct in CMYK because colors are represented in percentages from 0–100. This scale is easier to comprehend than RGB, which uses a scale of 0–255.

Correcting Image Contrast

To explain the concept of contrast, we first need to define some new terms related to the brightness of an image. The lightest area of an image that contains detail is called its "highlight"; the darkest area that contains detail is called the "shadow." The shades of gray between the highlights and shadows are the "midtones" (or "gamma") of the image.

Images contain three areas of brightness: highlights, midtones (gamma), and shadows.

Contrast, then, is defined as the difference between the highlight and the shadow. A low-contrast image looks washed out and lacks detail throughout the image. A high-contrast image lacks detail in the shadows and highlights; in some high-contrast images, the midtones are nearly nonexistent.

Low-contrast images (left) appear washed out, lacking overall detail.
High-contrast images (right) appear overexposed, lacking detail in the shadows and highlights.

Adjusting an image's contrast can reveal fine details in the shadows, and enhance details throughout the rest of the image.

By adjusting the tonal range so each channel uses the most available gray levels, the contrast is corrected to maintain detail in both the highlights and shadows.

The term "tonal range" refers to the number of shades of gray that exist between the lightest highlight and the darkest shadow of that image. A grayscale image can contain a maximum 256 possible shades of gray, as can each channel of a color image. To achieve the ideal contrast in an image, the tonal range should include as many levels of gray as are available.

Adjusting contrast is a three-step process:

- Determine the image's highlight areas (the lightest areas that contain detail).
- Determine the image's shadow areas (the darkest areas that contain detail).
- Adjust the *gamma* (the contrast in midtones of an image) to determine the proportion of darker tones to lighter tones.

Specular highlights are direct sources of light such as light bulbs or reflections on glass; specular highlights do not contain detail, so they should not be considered when identifying the highlight area of an image.

The reflection of light from the window is a specular highlight. It has no detail and should not be used as the defined highlight of an image.

The key to successful contrast adjustment is to find highlight and shadow points that maintain detail. After you have identified the target highlight and shadow areas of an image, you can use software to define the exact color values for those areas. Any color values beyond the defined highlight and shadow will be shifted to pure white and black, respectively. The values between the highlight and shadow will adjust accordingly, improving the overall tonal range and contrast of the image.

The target highlight in this image was defined with values of C:10 M:7 Y:7 K:0. Any area with values lower than those settings was dropped out (converted to pure white), destroying much of the highlight detail.

The target shadow in this image was selected in the cat's left ear, with values of C:70 M:70 Y:70 K:50. Any pixel with values greater than those targets was shifted to pure black, eliminating much of the detail in the shadow areas.

Correcting for Print: Printable Dots

When correcting images for print, defining highlight and shadow targets must account for the mechanics of the printing process. As we discussed in Chapter 5, the concepts of minimum printable dot and maximum printable dot are vital to accurately reproducing highlights and shadows on a commercial printing press. Remember that images are printed as a pattern of closely spaced dots called a "halftone." When viewed on the page, the dots create the illusion of continuous color. Different sizes of dots create different shades of color — larger dots create darker shades and smaller dots create lighter shades.

> If your images will be displayed electronically, you can safely work with pure RGB values for black and white. The darkest shadow is R:0 G:0 B:0, and the lightest highlight is R:255 G:255 B:255. When correcting images for print, there are additional considerations for defining highlight and shadow targets.

There is a lower limit to the size of dot that can be faithfully and consistently reproduced. A 1% dot, for example, *drops out* because it's too small for a mechanical press to create, so images with 1% dots specified will lack detail and contrast in their highlights. To avoid this problem, you need to specify the minimum printable dot for the highlights in CMYK images. There is some debate over the appropriate highlight setting because different presses and imaging equipment have varying capabilities, but to be sure your highlights will work on most printing equipment, you should typically define the highlight as C:5 M:3 Y:3 K:0.

> The larger percentage of cyan compensates for the hue contamination of cyan ink, resulting in a truly neutral highlight and shadow.

As you learned in Chapter 5, there are also upper limits to the amount of ink that can be printed on a given area of paper. The *total area coverage* (TAC) is the largest percentage of ink — determined by adding up the percentages of individual inks — that can be safely printed in a single area. As does the minimum printable dot, this value varies according to the specific ink/paper/press combination used for a given job. The limit for your particular combination dictates the shadow dot that you define. Unless your images will be printed in a newspaper, 290% is an acceptable shadow for most applications; you can safely define shadows as C:80 M:70 Y:70 K:70.

When you specify colors in a vector graphic or page-layout application, you can easily define the percentages of ink to avoid exceeding the TAC limit. In raster images, however, you cannot realistically examine and correct the ink percentages in every pixel. Shadow areas and dark colors in many digital images fall beyond the TAC limit, which should be corrected to avoid printing problems. When too much ink is printed, the result is a dark blob with no visible detail; heavy layers of ink also result in drying problems, smearing, and a number of other issues.

Two different techniques can be used, often in some combination, to correct for the inadequacies of mechanical printing: undercolor removal and gray component replacement.

UCR and GCR settings are applied when an image is converted from RGB to CMYK.

UNDERCOLOR REMOVAL

Using *undercolor removal* (UCR), black ink replaces cyan, magenta, and yellow inks in neutral areas (where CMY inks are present in equal percentages), especially in the shadows. This results in less ink to meet TAC limits, and provides greater depth in shadows. Because it uses less ink, UCR is commonly used for newsprint and uncoated stock, which generally have higher levels of dot gain.

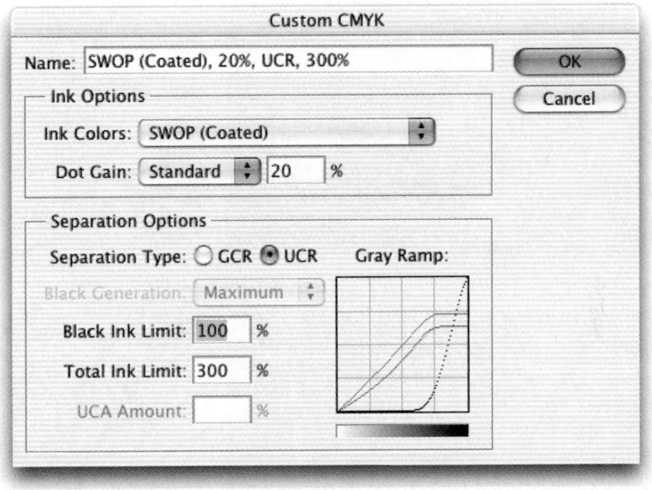

In the Photoshop Custom CMYK dialog box, the Gray Ramp shows how the four curves (C, M, Y, and K) will be generated using undercolor removal (UCR). The C, M, and Y curves flatten out at 75%; the K curve is flat until around 60, where it rises sharply to compensate for the flattened C, M, and Y curves.

GRAY COMPONENT REPLACEMENT

Using *gray component replacement* (GCR), black ink replaces portions of cyan, magenta, and yellow ink in colored areas as well as in neutral areas. GCR separations tend to reproduce dark, saturated colors better than UCR separations.

Light GCR.

Medium GCR.

Maximum GCR.

The black separations show the effects of different levels of GCR. Using Light GCR (top), black ink is most pronounced in the shadow areas. Medium GCR (middle) extends the black ink into the midtones of the image. Maximum GCR (bottom) extends even into the quartertones.

When you use GCR, you can also apply *undercolor addition* (UCA) to add a smaller percentage of cyan, magenta, and yellow back into the shadow areas. By itself, black ink appears dull and flat. UCA compensates for the loss of ink density in neutral shadows, producing richer shadows than you can achieve with only black ink.

> You can choose from the GCR settings built into Photoshop, or you can create custom GCR curves.

Adobe Photoshop Correction Tools

It is impossible to discuss color correction without discussing Adobe Photoshop — the industry-standard application for editing digital images. While Photoshop users debate about which color-correction tool is best, there is no "one perfect tool" for adjusting images; the "best" tool depends on the job that needs to be done.

THE INFO PALETTE

The Info palette and Eyedropper/Color Sampler tool are the two most important Photoshop tools for evaluating and correcting color. You can change the Info palette's options to show both RGB and CMYK values of a given area. This allows you to quickly identify problems regardless of which color mode you are more comfortable using. In fact, this is one area of color correction for which absolutely no artistic judgment is required. The numbers in the Info palette — not your eyes — identify the incorrect gray balance.

The only human judgment required to correct gray balance is to identify the gray areas of the image. These are obvious in many cases, but some middle-key images might not have an obvious highlight or shadow point, so choosing the midtone requires a bit more care. If an image has a heavy color cast, the white highlights may appear yellow or cyan, making it more difficult to choose a "neutral" area.

Moving the Eyedropper tool around an image can help to identify the neutral areas. When the RGB values almost match, you have found what is likely to be a neutral gray. Of course, the equal values may be the result of the problems that exist. This is when human judgment comes into play. Ask yourself two questions: What is the object that shows up as numerically equal? Does the viewer expect that object to be neutral?

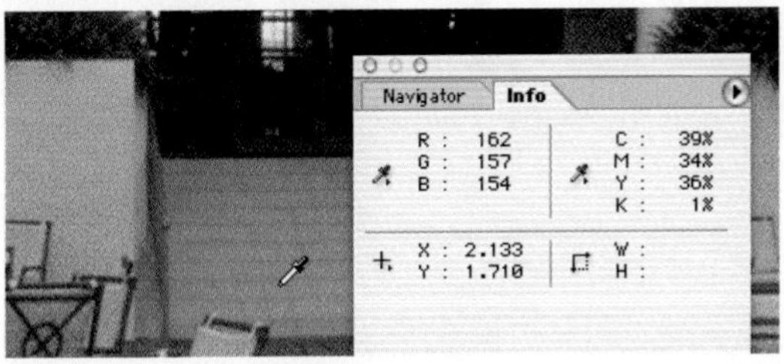

In the previous image, the Info palette shows approximately equal CMY percentages, which indicates a reddish color cast because the cyan is not high enough to correct for ink impurities. The RGB values confirm that there is slightly more red in the area, while green and blue are approximately the same. Before correcting, you need to determine if this is truly a neutral area. Are concrete stairs usually gray? Is the red cast part of the image, or should it be corrected? The answer to the first question is, "Yes, we can expect concrete stairs to be gray," so the answer to the second question is, "The reddish cast should be corrected." Correcting the gray balance of this image should remove the red cast in the midtones.

BRIGHTNESS/CONTRAST

The Photoshop Brightness/Contrast command offers very basic adjustment and control over an image. You can increase or decrease the brightness and contrast sliders to apply changes.

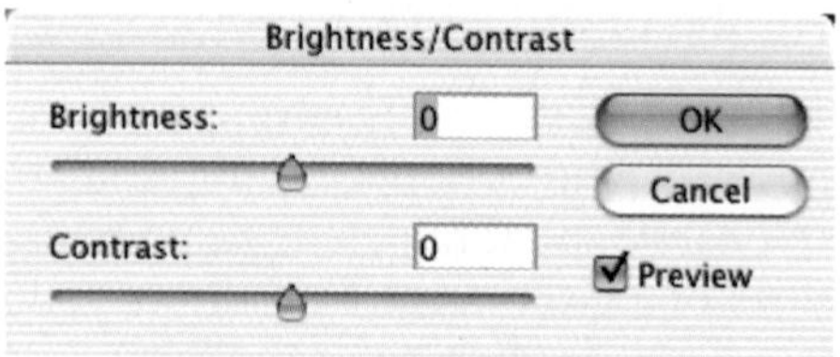

Changes made using the Brightness/Contrast tool affect the entire image. This option is useful for very minor correction, and can create artistic effects by blowing the brightness and contrast out of proportion. For complex color correction, or in situations where you need finer control over the changes, however, you should use other Photoshop tools.

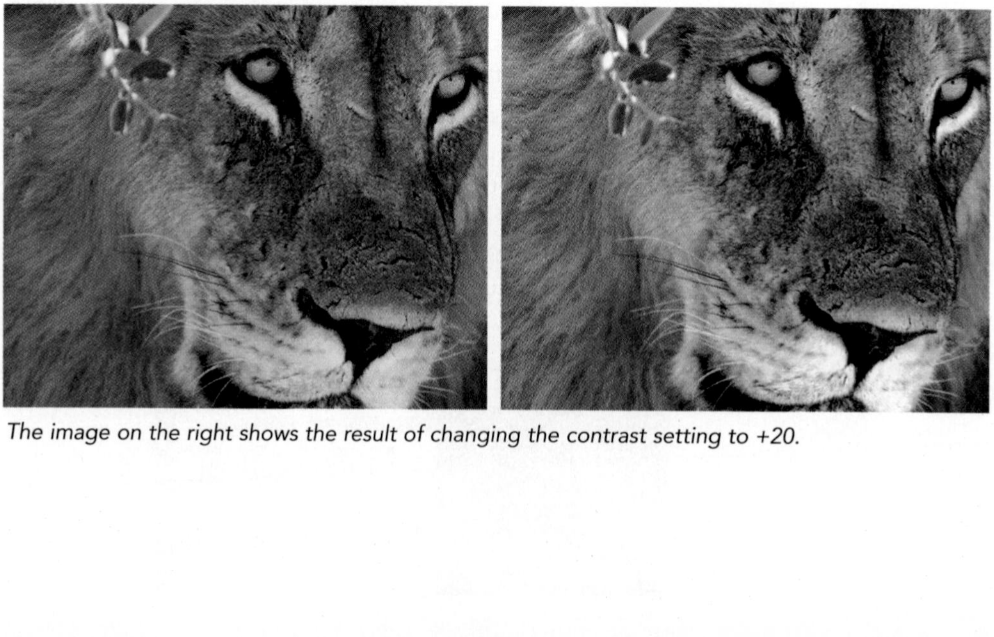

The image on the right shows the result of changing the contrast setting to +20.

LEVELS

The Photoshop Levels tool allows you to adjust highlight, shadow, and gamma settings individually. In addition, you can work on all the channels in a document at once, or on an individual channel. The most dominant feature of the Levels dialog box is the *histogram*, the graph in the center of the box. The histogram represents the distribution of pixels for each channel, or for the entire image.

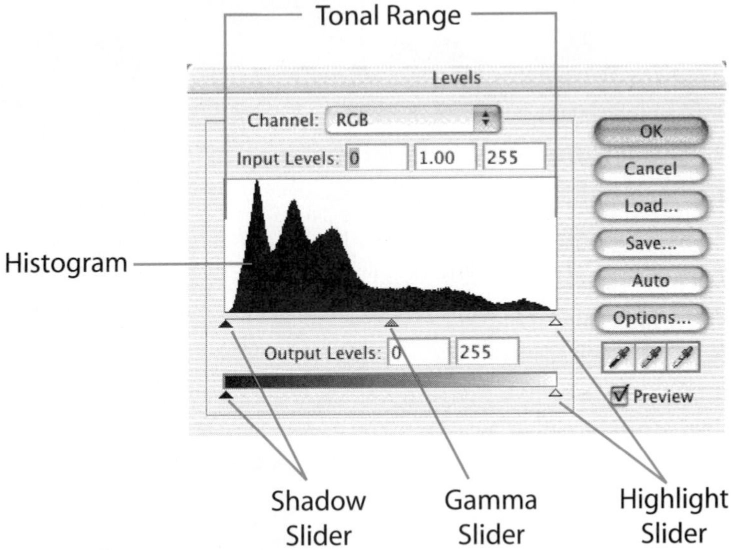

In a low-contrast image, the histogram is compressed within the available area of the graph; white space to the left and/or right of the histogram indicates gray levels that aren't being used in the image.

The low-contrast image and the associated histogram show that a significant number of possible tones are not used.

The histogram for a typical high-contrast image extends across the entire possible range, but shows large concentrations near each end of the histogram with little or no variation in the middle.

The histogram of a high-contrast image shows large concentrations in the highlight and shadow areas, but little variation in the middle range.

Controlling Input and Output Levels

Within the Levels dialog box, there are two sets of sliders that allow you to control input levels and output levels. Input sliders reflect the shades or levels that exist in the original image. Output sliders reflect the shades or levels that will be used in the adjusted image; the Output scale is set by default to include the entire range of available gray levels (0–255). When you click OK in the Levels dialog box, input levels are mapped to the appropriate shade on the output scale.

Both sets (input and output) have a black slider for adjusting the shadows in an image and a white slider to adjust highlights. The Input Levels bar also has a third slider (the gray triangle) for adjusting gamma or midtones. You can change input and output levels by moving the sliders, entering actual values in the boxes above the slider sets, or by using the eyedroppers to select the brightest and darkest points in the image.

To increase the contrast of an image, the input levels should be adjusted so the darkest areas of the image are reproduced with the darkest possible shade, and the lightest part of the image is reproduced

Automatic Correction

Photoshop includes options to automatically correct levels and contrast. These are, as the word suggests, automatic — they allow absolutely no user interaction or control. They can, however, noticeably improve an image, and are the "better than nothing" option.

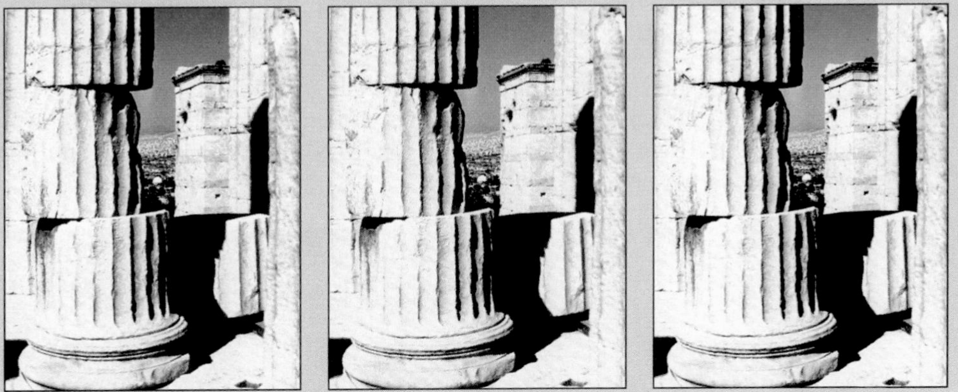

The image was corrected using Photoshop Auto Levels (left); by manually adjusting the combined CMYK histogram (middle); and by manually adjusting the histograms of individual channels (right).

with the lightest possible shade. This is as simple as dragging the Input Shadow (black) slider to the right and dragging the Input Highlight (white) slider to the left until they touch the first discernible rise in the histogram. Any pixels that exist to the left of the Input Shadow slider will then reproduced as solid black; no detail will be visible in those areas of the image. Any pixels that exist to the right of the Input Highlight slider will be reproduced as pure white; no detail will be visible in those areas either. This simple adjustment extends the colors in the image to take advantage of all 256 possible shades of gray, and improves the overall image contrast.

To decrease contrast in an image, you can adjust the Output sliders. This effectively compresses the range of possible shades that can be reproduced, forcing all areas of the image into a smaller tonal range. Input shades that were originally set to 0 are reproduced at the value of the Output Shadow slider; input shades originally set to 255 are output at the value of the Output Highlight slider.

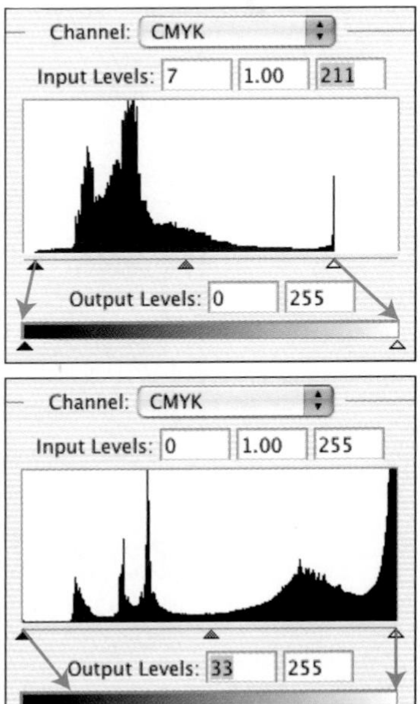

Input levels are remapped to the appropriate output levels when you make changes in the Levels dialog box.

Manipulating Midtones

The Input Gamma (middle) slider allows you to control the proportion of darker shades to lighter shades in the midtones of an image. Dragging the slider to the left (increasing gamma) increases the proportion of lighter grays in the image. This effectively increases the contrast in lighter areas, but it also lightens the entire image and decreases contrast in the darker areas.

Dragging the slider to the right (decreasing gamma) extends the tonal range of the darker grays; this allows those areas of the image to be reproduced with a larger range of shades, which increases the contrast in the darker areas.

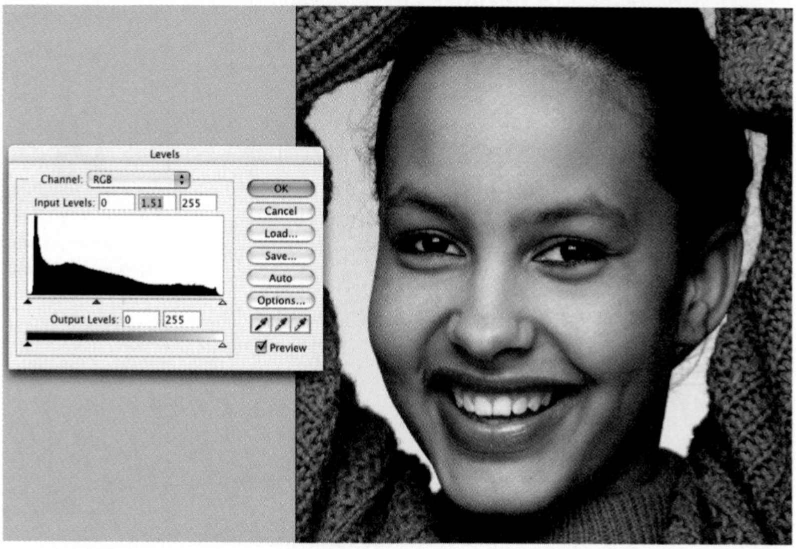

Notice that the entire image is lightened by increased gamma.

Notice the darkening effect of decreased gamma.

COLOR BALANCE

Color Balance is another basic correction tool. It's easy to use, but lacks the fine adjustments necessary for proper color correction. The Color Balance adjustment is best used when correcting an overall color cast of an image.

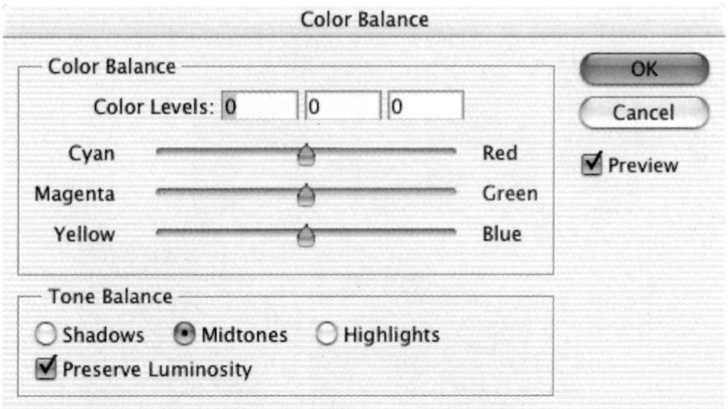

This dialog box presents three sliders, one for each pair of complementary colors. You can choose to adjust the highlights, shadows, or midtones of an image by selecting the appropriate radio button. Dragging the color sliders adjusts the color in the selected area of the image. The Preserve Luminosity check box ensures that only the colors shift, leaving the tonal balance of the image unchanged. Color Balance is well suited for special effects such as adjusting artificial textural backgrounds created in Photoshop, but it shouldn't be used for general color correction.

By adjusting the Color Balance settings, some of the green cast can be removed (right). Notice, however, that some of the highlight detail has been lost.

VARIATIONS

From the Photoshop Variations dialog box, you can make adjustments based strictly on visible information. Variations is a quick and easy adjustment technique, but it lacks the fine control of other correction methods. This tool is particularly useful for adjusting color in Web images; for print images, Variations can be used for basic correction such as removing overall color cast. Remember, however, that correcting for print should be based more on numbers than on what you see on your monitor.

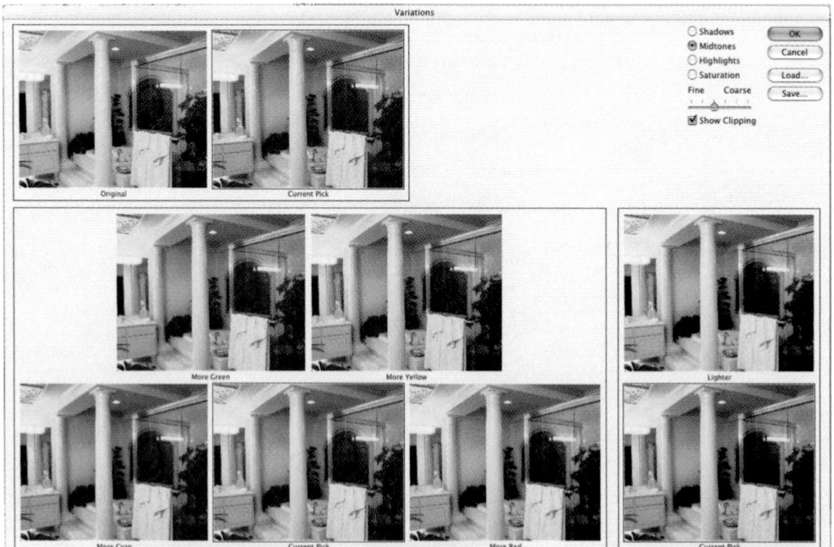

In the Variations window, you can see a preview of the original image compared to the result of any changes you make. The lower-left area of the window shows the result of adding any single primary color to the part of the image selected with the radio buttons (Shadows, Midtones, Highlights, or Saturation). You can also darken or lighten the image by clicking an option in the right column of the window.

If the upper-right image (which adds yellow) looked better than the center image, clicking the upper-right image would move it to the center, and then recolor the surrounding images. You could then decide to add some magenta, which would move that image to the center.

If you understand the interaction of primary colors, the Variations tool can be used to correct color cast.

HUE/SATURATION

Hue/Saturation adjustment can be extremely useful in some situations. For example, an improperly calibrated scanner can sometimes shift the colors around the color wheel, making cyan appear too green, magenta too blue, and yellow too red. A quick adjustment with the Hue/Saturation command can easily correct this problem.

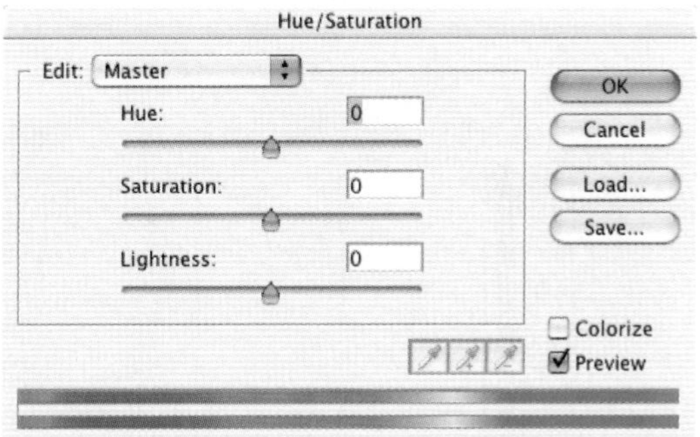

The Hue/Saturation tool can be used to adjust the overall saturation or lightness of an image, or to adjust individual colors in an image. For example, you can use this tool to turn a lemon into a lime; we know a designer who turned a yellow Lamborghini red to satisfy a client.

SELECTIVE COLOR REPLACEMENT

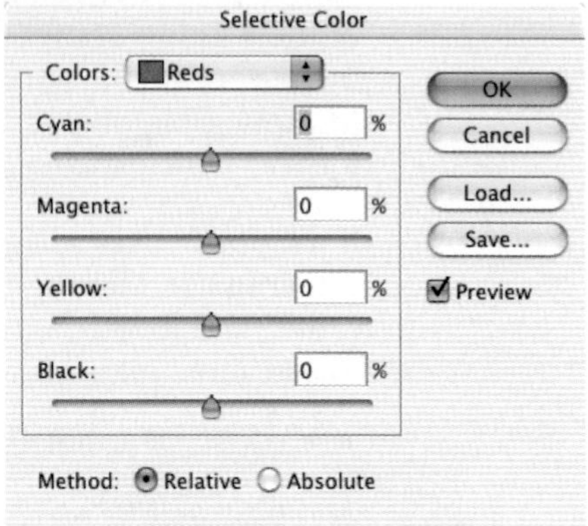

The Selective Color controls allow you to edit the tonal values in the neutrals, blacks, whites, or individual primary colors — without affecting other color components of the image.

If a red car looks too magenta, you probably want to remove magenta from the image to produce a truer red. Unfortunately, magenta is a component of blue, as well as a color in its own right. If you reduce the amount of magenta, you might give your deep blue sky a greenish cast.

Selective Color allows you to adjust the components of red shades without affecting other areas of the image. You can, for example, adjust the magenta component of red to correct the car without affecting the magenta component in blue values of the sky. Selective Color allows you to adjust the actual ink values, and can isolate and adjust the blacks and whites in your image.

CURVES

The Curves tool is the most powerful color-correction tool in Photoshop. From the Curves dialog box, you can make very fine adjustments to the color of the entire composite image or to individual color channels. You can alter one channel at a time by making appropriate choices from the Channel menu. The eyedroppers in the Curves dialog box allow you to define the highlight and shadow targets of an image. The three icons signify the Set Black Point or Shadow eyedropper (filled with black), the Set Midpoint or Midtone eyedropper (filled with gray), and the Set White Point or Highlight eyedropper (filled with white).

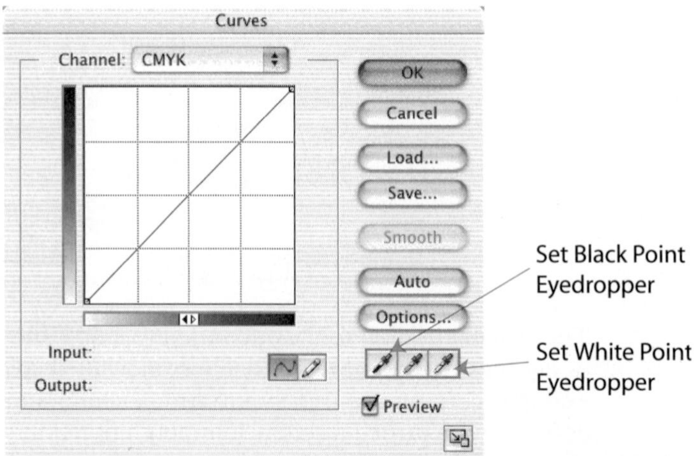

Double-clicking any of these eyedroppers opens the Color Picker, where you can specify the dot percentage of each ink (cyan, magenta, yellow, and black) in the highlights, midtones, and shadows.

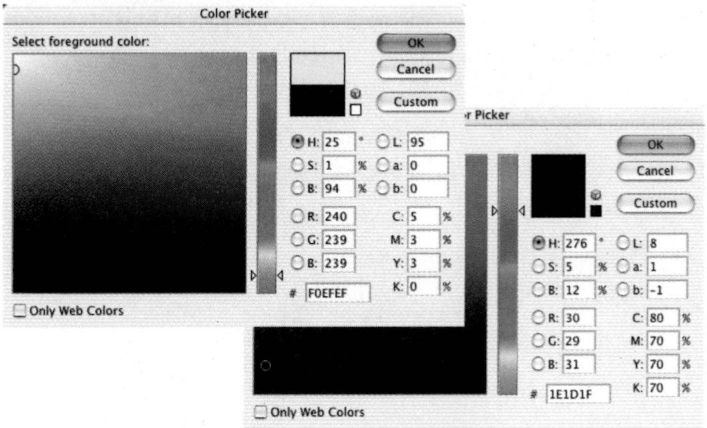

Setting standard values for an image's highlight point (C:5 M:3 Y:3 K:0) and shadow point (C:80 M:70 Y:70 K:70) in the Color Picker.

Once you have defined the highlight and shadow targets, it is fairly simple to apply those settings. When an eyedropper is active in the Curves dialog box, clicking the image applies the value of that eyedropper to the area of the image on which you clicked.

A straight diagonal line in the Curves graph represents the existing color in the image. The horizontal axis represents the input color value and the vertical axis represents the output color value. The lower-left point of the line is the minimum value (0), and the upper-right point is the maximum value (255 for RGB images and 100 for CMYK images).

The grayscale bars to the left and directly below the Curves diagram indicate the levels of gray that exist. If the image is RGB, the grayscale begins at black (R:0 G:0 B:0) and continues to white (R:255 G:255 B:255). For a CMYK image, the grayscale begins at white (C:0 M:0 Y:0 K:0) and continues to black (C:100 M:100 Y:100 K:100).

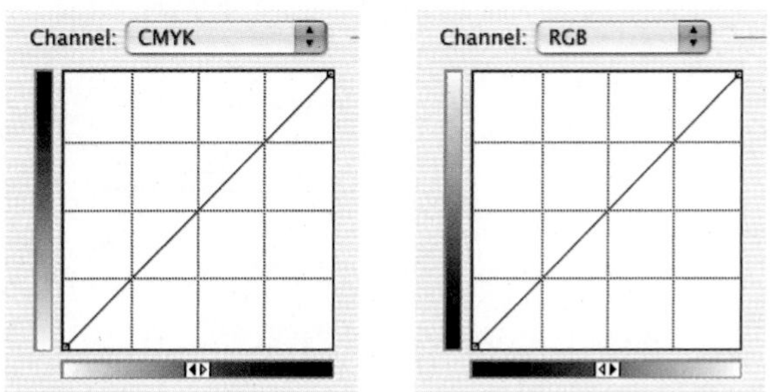

The curves for CMYK (left) and RGB (right) images. The curves function in the same way, but have opposite start and end points.

To change the RGB curve to begin at white, you can click the opposing arrows in the middle of the lower grayscale. This reverses the curve (and the grayscales), and allows you to more easily relate an RGB image to a CMYK image that will be printed.

Remember, the additive colors (RGB) combine to create pure white, while the subtractive colors (CMY) at full strength combine to create pure black.

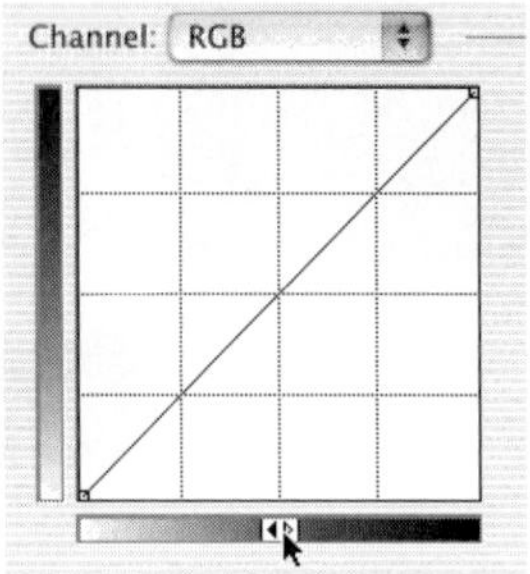

Understanding Curves

To effectively use curves, you need to understand how the shape of the curve affects the image. When you begin, the curve is a straight line from white to black. This means that a pixel with a value of 0 will be reproduced as 0, a pixel with a value of 100 will be reproduced as 100, and all pixels in between 0 and 100 have the same correlation.

You can adjust the curve by clicking on the line to add an anchor point, then dragging the point to a different location. The Input and Output fields show the original location of the point compared to the final location of the point. In the following image, the active (solid) point shows that any pixel originally set at 65% will be output at 76%. Other areas will be adjusted accordingly so the curve remains a curve instead of becoming a series of random dots.

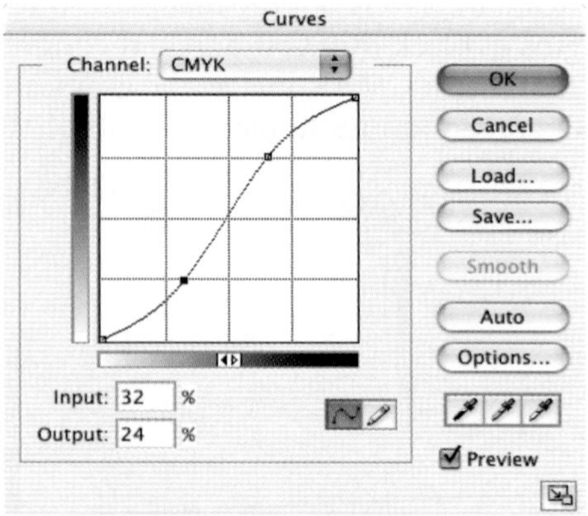

The 65% dot is in the darker range of midtones technically called "three-quartertones." Making this adjustment to the curves considerably darkens the three-quartertones of the image.

Clicking on the other point activates it, and shows the Input and Output values for that point. The Input value of 35% is reduced to the Output value of 25%, which lightens the lighter midtones (called "quartertones") of the image. Other quartertone values are adjusted to the shape of the resultant curve.

Adjusting the curves also affects image contrast. The most important thing to remember is that the steeper the curve, the greater the contrast in that area of the image. Conversely, flattening an area of the curve decreases contrast.

Points to Remember about Curves

Curves are very powerful tools and can be intimidating. To simplify their use and make them less daunting, keep these points in mind:

- Aim for neutral grays.
- You can adjust the curve for an entire image, or adjust the individual curve for each channel of the image.
- The bottom grayscale shows the Input value, the left grayscale shows the Output value.
- Changes made to one area of a curve affect all other areas. You can minimize the effect on other areas of the curve by defining additional points.

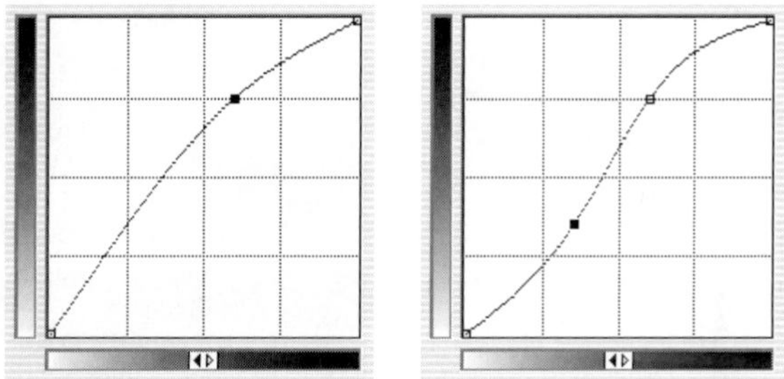

If you want to change the three-quartertones, you can minimize the change in the highlights and quartertones by adding an additional point to the curve (right).

- The steeper the curve, the greater the contrast.
- Increasing contrast in one area inherently decreases the contrast in other areas.

In the images on the following page, the curve between the quartertone and three-quartertone is flattened. Original values between 25% and 75% are compressed into the tonal range of 38%–60%. The original range of 50 possible shades of gray is compressed into 22 possible shades of gray, which decreases contrast. The original values from 0%–25% can now be reproduced in the tonal range of 0%–38%, increasing the tonal range in those areas, and thus increasing contrast. Similarly, the original values from 75%–100% are now extended to 60%–100%, again increasing tonal range and contrast.

The original image.

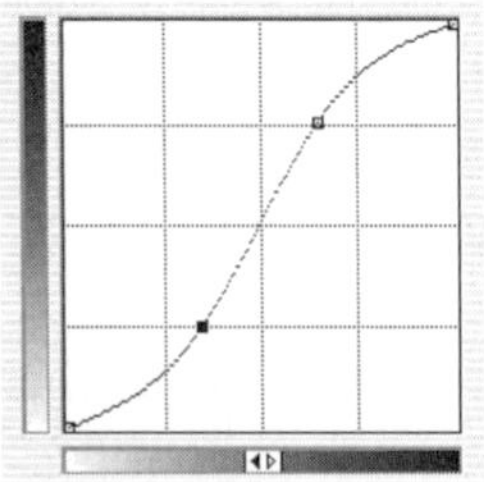

Increasing the curve in the midtones improves the middle range, but flattens contrast in the highlights and shadows.

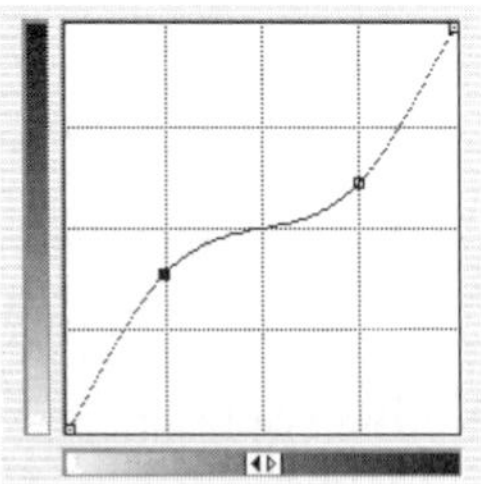

Flattening the curve in the midtone range improves contrast in the highlights and shadows, but minimizes the contrast in midtones.

Conclusion

As with many other skills, it takes time and practice to master image color-correction techniques. Understanding the relationship between brightness and contrast, and how these two values affect the quality of reproduction in digital images, is the first and possibly the most critical factor in creating a high-quality image. An image that has too much contrast (a "sharp" image) or not enough contrast (a "flat" image) translates to an unsatisfactory print.

A basic understanding of color theory (specifically complementary color) is the foundation of accurate color correction; Photoshop's Info palette and Eyedropper tool are by far the most important tools when correcting color. Effective color correction relies on the numbers, rather than what you think you see on your monitor. As you gain experience in correcting images, you will be better able to predict the corrections required to achieve the best possible output.

CHAPTER 8

Color Proofing

Any graphics job should be proofed at least twice — once before being sent to the printer, and once after the printer prepares the files for output.

There are a number of available proofing options, from inexpensive inkjet proofs to high-end commercial proofing systems. Generally, designers work with inkjet, laser, and soft proofs during the file-creation process, because it's easy and inexpensive to generate multiple copies of these options. Higher-end proofs, which are more expensive to produce, are usually restricted to the final *contract proof* just before a job moves into production.

There are two broad categories of proofing devices: analog and digital. Analog proofs are made from imaged film, which is produced almost exclusively on an *imagesetter*. Digital proofs are made directly from the digital data in your files, and no film is used in the process.

Desktop or *layout* proofs are typically made with a black-and-white laser or color inkjet printer. These are the versions of your document that you print 74 times during the design phase to make sure all the elements are included exactly as they are supposed to be. Desktop proofs serve several purposes. Their primary role is to check overall layout including page balance, element positions, and relative placement of color. Layout proofs are also useful for editing and proofreading text. Many designers also choose to share these proofs with their clients for approval during the development stage.

Contract proofs are a second type of proof. This category includes anything that is presented for final approval, whether it's produced on a desktop inkjet printer or as film from an imagesetter. The contract proof should be signed by anyone with a financial stake in the outcome of the job — the designer, the client, and the printer. When a contract proof is approved and signed, it has several uses.

Foremost, it provides a benchmark or goal for press operators to match on the press. Think of a proof as a blueprint. When the press operator is conducting makeready, the press controls are adjusted until the printed color matches the signed proof.

Common problems like typos, missing text, image errors, and font replacement are easy to catch if you actually look at your contract proofs. Regardless, many designers (even the most experienced ones) often sign off after only a casual glance at proofs. It pays to be diligent; when problems occur — notice we say *when* instead of *if* — the signed contract proof is your legal support.

Even with a signed proof to back you up, you should always consider the implications of disclaiming any responsibility for errors, especially when dealing with upset clients. Don't expect much return business if you make a habit of answering, "Sorry, you signed off on it!"

Conversely, if a problem is introduced at the printer, don't call your printer screaming. If you approach the situation rationally, most reputable printers will bend over backwards to correct their mistakes. If you immediately call and threaten lawsuits, you probably won't find the printer so accommodating.

Second, contract proofs provide legal protection in case something goes wrong. If your client discovers that her name is misspelled on her new business cards, you can check to see if the contract proof shows the same error. When a client signs a proof, she is saying, "I accept this as it appears on this page." If she approves a job with errors, she can't hold you financially responsible.

Not only can contract proofs protect you from clients, they also protect you from paying for printer errors. When you approve a contract proof, you are telling the printer exactly what you expect to see on the final press sheet. If a job is printed and all the yellows look orange, you can compare the final result to the contract proof. If the proof had nice, yellow bananas, then it's the printer's responsibility to correct the problem and absorb the cost. If you didn't really look at the contract proof before signing it, you may have to live with orange bananas — or pay to reprint the job.

When you review contract proofs, it's your responsibility to carefully evaluate every aspect of them; errors not caught at this stage will appear in the final product.

- Check the order of pages. Clearly indicate any that are missing or out of order.
- Check page geometry for trim size, correct margins, and any folds.
- Check that all elements — images, characters, symbols, illustrations, lines, and so on — appear correctly in the proof.
- Check for correct typeface, font substitutions, and distorted or broken type.
- Never overlook the obvious. Check names, addresses, phone numbers, Web and email addresses, and other familiar items that are often overlooked or assumed to be correct.

- Check image detail and resolution.
- Check that any spot colors are separated properly.
- Compare color reproductions to the original photos or slides if possible.
- Check neutral areas for color cast.
- Mark color changes specifically. Indicate color adjustments as "+red" or "–yellow," and tone changes as "±lightness," "±contrast," and so forth.

> If there are errors in any images that you scanned yourself, you have two choices. You can either make any necessary changes yourself (and pay for another proof), or pay for the printer to make the changes (and *still* pay for another proof).

Return corrected proofs to the printer; you can ask for another proof to be made to check that the corrections were incorporated, or approve the proofs with the condition that the requested changes are made.

Proofing Standards and Expectations

Each type of printing technology has industry standards and specifications that are accepted by the majority of North American printers:

- Specification for Web Offset Publications (SWOP) is the standard for web-offset printing.
- General Requirements for Applications in Commercial Offset Lithography (GRACoL) is often used for sheetfed-offset printing.
- Specifications for Newsprint Advertising Production (SNAP) is commonly used for newspaper printing.

Color proofs are made with one of these specific standards as its target. For web-offset (and sometimes gravure) printing, proofs are made to SWOP specifications. For sheetfed-offset, many printers make the proof to reflect the capabilities of their presses rather than to the GRACoL specification because printing conditions vary widely on sheetfed presses. Whatever standard is applied, the proofs are designed to reflect the way colors will appear on a specific ink/paper/press combination.

ACCURATE COLOR VS. PLEASING COLOR

There are two basic goals when designing with color: *matching color* and *pleasing color*. In some cases, colors in the printed job have to match the colors of another object exactly. This is often the case with corporate branding, where logos and packaging are supposed to be a very specific color. Product marketing also relies on matching color. The colors in a catalog have to accurately reflect what the consumer is purchasing; when customers order blue t-shirts, they expect them to be blue and not purple.

For other printing jobs, your goal is to make something that looks good — pleasing color. In these cases, it doesn't matter if the blue in a sky matches the blue in a book cover, the blue sky just has to look good. When your goal is pleasing color, you have a lot more flexibility and a lot more room for manipulation.

VIEWING COLOR PROOFS

Even if proofs are created to an accepted industry standard, some colors can look different depending on the lighting (called "metamerism"). From a strictly scientific perspective, color proofs should be viewed in a light booth with controlled (5000K) illumination to avoid this problem. If you evaluate proofs in your office under fluorescent or incandescent lighting, you might not get an accurate impression of the color in the job. Another reason for using standard lighting is to ensure that viewing conditions are consistent. Using controlled lighting, you know that you, your client, and your printer are all seeing the same color.

Many design professionals, however, prefer to proof color in the same light that will eventually be used to view the final product. Stores, outdoor venues, and (of course) people's homes aren't usually equipped with 5000K viewing booths. To simulate real viewing conditions, designers often take their color proofs outside, into stores, or into dimly lit living rooms to evaluate color the way it will be seen by the consumer.

There is validity to each approach, and it is ultimately your decision which you will use. If you need an exact color match, you may be better off using the standard viewing booth. If you are only aiming for something that "looks good" — regardless of what the actual color is — you might want to move the proof into its eventual destination before you evaluate the color.

Analog Proofs

Analog proofs are made whenever a job is imaged to film. Because the film used for making the proofs is also used to expose printing plates, what you see on the proof will end up on the plate exactly — analog proofs are very accurate. They also provide great detail because they show the halftone dot structure of images. If you make changes or corrections to the proof, a new set of film and proofs must be made.

One disadvantage of analog proofs is the late stage of production at which the proofs are made, usually right before a job is ready to go on press. Also, film and film-based proofing are very expensive, labor-intensive, and time-consuming; multiple rounds of changes and reproofs can be extremely expensive

BLUELINES AND BROWNLINES

A *blueline* or *brownline* (also called "Dylux," which is DuPont's brand of proofing material) is an analog proof generated by exposing a special paper with the same film that will be used to create the plates for the press. These proofs are exposed, then trimmed and folded to represent the layout of the finished job.

Bluelines are inexpensive and extremely accurate proofs; they are excellent for checking copy, trim, bleeds, folds, and register. In general, you should request a blueline for any job that is being printed with conventional offset lithography. A blueline is the best way to check the accuracy of a job with folds.

To create a blueline proof, special ultraviolet-sensitive paper is exposed using the job film. Clear areas in the film produce blue or brown areas on the paper; solid areas of the film do not allow light to pass through, so the paper is not exposed.

These proofs, when finished, are always one color — blue or brown (hence the name). That doesn't mean that your job will print in blue or brown. These proofs are solely for the purpose of checking layout and placement, not for checking color or image detail (although you will certainly be able to notice poor image quality). Color jobs should be proofed with both a blueline and color proof.

LAMINATE PROOFS

Laminate proofs are the most common type of analog proofs. For each color separation, a light-sensitive color dye sheet is laminated to a base material with heat and pressure, the film is placed on top, then it's exposed in a vacuum frame using a strong ultraviolet lamp. After exposure, the proof is chemically processed to removed the exposed areas of dye. This is repeated until all color separations have been imaged and fixed to the base sheet.

With some laminate proofing systems, you can use the actual paper stock that is specified for the job; other systems use a special base material designed to simulate most types of printing papers.

Common laminate proof systems are Kodak Polychrome Graphics MatchPrint III, Agfa PressMatch, Fuji ColorArt, and DuPont WaterProof. Some require chemical processing and some don't, but all of them are capable of producing an accurate proof of your work. All use process-color (CMYK) dye sheets, and most offer spot-color dye sheets for proofing a limited range of PANTONE colors. Some even offer metallic sheets for proofing metallic inks, but these are generally limited to silver and gold.

OVERLAY PROOFS

Overlay proofs or *color keys* follow the same basic concept as laminate proofs. The primary difference is that the exposed dye sheets are not laminated to the base material. Rather, they are taped on the top edge, one on top of the other, to a base paper sheet. Overlay proofs allow you to proof on virtually any substrate, which is useful if you are printing on a colored or textured paper. They are sometimes called "progressive" because you can lift the sheets and see the progression of process colors that will build your image.

The only overlay proofing system still in use is the Kodak Polychrome Graphics Color Key system. Overlay proofs are less expensive than laminate proofs, but the color is not as accurate. If your goal is pleasing color rather than matching color, an overlay proof can be an acceptable contract proof.

TONER PROOFS

If you need to proof a spot color that isn't available in a laminate system, you'll probably need to make a toner proof. In a toner proof, film is exposed to a base sheet; where exposed, the base is sensitized and becomes sticky. The proof maker wipes on a fine powdered toner that is mixed to represent the desired ink, and the toner sticks to the sensitized areas of the base. To proof additional colors, another base sheet is laminated to the one that's already been processed. The final step is to laminate the layered base sheets to a sheet of paper.

Toner proofs are very messy to make. They often show swirls from the motion of the proof maker's wiping actions. Toner proofing systems have largely disappeared, with the exception of DuPont Cromalin, so finding someone to make one might be a challenge. An alternative is to use a laminate proof, substituting a close-enough spot color to stand in for the color that you're trying to proof.

Digital Proofs

If a job is imaged directly to printing plates (computer-to-plate or CTP), or will be printed on a digital press, digital proofing is the only option because no film is used in the printing process. Digital proofs are produced by a digitally driven imaging device and are typically delivered finished from the proofer, needing no further processing.

> Analog proofs start out as digital files, and the film used to make them is digitally imaged, but they're not considered digital proofs.

Digital proofs have a unique set of advantages and disadvantages. Digital proofs can be made much earlier in the production cycle, which means problems can be identified and corrected long before the job is ready to go to press. Some digital proofing devices are affordable enough that designers and ad agencies can place them in-house, making high-quality proofs available quickly. The cost of consumables to produce digital proofs is usually lower than that of analog proofs, and there's little labor involved.

> It's cheaper and faster to correct errors in a direct-to-plate job as long as the error is caught before the plates are imaged; in a film-based job, changes require expensive new film, along with the cost of a new proof.

Disadvantages of digital proofs are less well-defined. Many digital proofers can't reproduce the halftone dot patterns that are present on the final plates. In addition, the digital data used to make a digital proof is not always the same data used to make the final plates — "Just one tiny change!" — which introduces room for error.

DIGITAL HALFTONE PROOFS

Most digital proofers produce continuous-tone proofs that look like photographic prints, which means there is no visible halftone dot pattern. The Kodak Approval and Polaroid PolaProof are two halftone digital proofers in fairly widespread use. (Polaroid Corporation liquidated in 2002, but the proofing-systems division is still in business.)

These machines — and their consumables — are extremely expensive, but they produce very high-quality proofs that can be imaged to a selection of paper stocks instead of only a special base material like some analog proofs. The disadvantage to these devices (other than cost) is the limited proof size; they can generally handle no larger than a four-page imposition.

INKJET PROOFS

Inkjet is the fastest-growing type of proofing. These devices — just like the one that is probably on your desktop — use inkjet technology to create continuous-tone images and full, pleasing color. Wide-format inkjet printers are commonly used for large pages and multiple-page impositions; smaller devices are used for standard page and image proofing. Many inkjet proofers use six or seven colors of ink to extend their gamuts; this produces a closer match to press conditions. It also allows proofing for hifi or Hexachrome jobs.

To function as an accurate proofing device, an inkjet printer is driven by a color-managed print server, using ICC profiles to simulate a given printing condition (SWOP, GRACoL, and so on). Any inkjet printer has a much larger color gamut than any printing press, so the profile is necessary, essentially, to tell the inkjet printer to not be so colorful. This is the only way to accurately simulate the color-reproduction characteristics of typical offset printing.

There are many brands of wide-format inkjet proofers; Epson, Hewlett-Packard, and Encad are among the most popular. There are even more brands of color print servers, including (but not limited to) EFI, Best Color, Creo, and Kodak Polychrome Graphics.

Also available are some large-format systems that print in one color (black), and have a mechanism that flips over the sheet so the back can be printed. These devices use a lightweight paper that can be easily folded and trimmed like a blueline. Only one color is used because the lightweight papers can't absorb the amount of ink sprayed on the surface in full-color inkjet printing.

Smaller inkjet printers such as the HP 20PS, Epson 7600, and others aren't capable of the eight-page impositions of wide-format machines, but they are much less expensive. These are the ones typically found in design firms and ad agencies.

DYE PROOFS

Dye-sublimation or "dye-sub" printers are another type of continuous-tone digital proofer. The term "sublimation" describes the process of transferring dye from a donor sheet to a specially-treated paper stock (although technically, the process is properly called "dye diffusion" rather than sublimation).

As with an inkjet, the color print server driving one of these machines must be configured to simulate a printing condition, typically with an ICC output profile. Fuji Pictro, the Kodak DCP series, and Imation Rainbow are examples of dye-sub proofing systems. Dye-sub proofers are faster than inkjets, and produce very high quality. Disadvantages are that they are limited to layouts no larger than 11 × 17 in., and the consumables are expensive.

Press Proofs and Press Checks

The most accurate — and most expensive — type of proof is made on a printing press using the same paper stock and inks specified for the job. This is basically the same as doing the final press run in a very small quantity. Press proofs are expensive because of the costs associated with making plates, setting up the press, and loading paper. Press proofs are usually made when a large quantity of proofs is needed, or when the final run is very large and the cost to reprint would be prohibitive.

Press proofs can also be created on a *proofing press*, which uses the actual plates for the job but is not the same press that will be used for the final press run. Proofing presses are usually separate presses on the shop floor that are only used to print proofs.

A third option for creating press proofs is the newest generation of digital presses such as the Indigo. Digital-printing technology allows fast turnaround for digital-color files, and produces high-quality proofs. For a job that will be printed digitally, using the digital press to create a proof allows you to preview *exactly* what the final job will look like.

The best possible alternative to a press proof is a *press check*. During a press check, you (and possibly your client) will be present in the pressroom when your job is printed, so you'll be able to say when the press sheets are showing acceptable color.

Some printers, and especially the press operators, discourage client press checks because so many people don't understand the technical capabilities of the process. We hear countless stories of clients asking press operators to make a blue car green, or make a red shirt pink, or some other change that should have been made in the color-correction stage. It is not surprising, then, that some printers actually charge extra if you want to attend the press check — purely to avoid the unnecessary interference. Because you now understand the science and mechanics of color reproduction, you should be able to avoid making requests that make press operators cringe.

Soft Proofing

With the availability of precise CRT and LCD color monitors and the use of a colorimeter or spectrophotometer to measure their output, it is now possible to view accurate proofs on a computer display — known as "soft proofing" because no physical medium is used.

The most common method for soft proofing is to create a PDF file, which is viewable in Adobe Reader and Adobe Acrobat. Some other types of soft proofing, such as Creo VPS (Virtual Proofing System), render the job to large bitmap files that accurately represent the data that will be sent to an imagesetter or platesetter; viewing these files requires a special viewing application, and they're primarily intended to communicate layout rather than color.

Older LCD monitors didn't have the same range of color and tone as CRT monitors, and the image appearance wasn't accurate unless you were directly in front of the monitor. The technology has progressed — LCD monitors now are sharper, take up less space, and consume far less electricity than CRTs; they no longer have the directional viewing issues of older models.

Monitors suitable for soft proofing are available from Sony, Barco, LaCie, and other vendors. Apple's 20-in. Cinema LCD display has been approved by SWOP, Inc. as accurately representing standard SWOP printing conditions — the first LCD monitor to be approved by SWOP.

Some Internet-based soft-proofing products allow you to view proofs through a Web browser, although most Web browsers don't support color management. Only Microsoft Internet Explorer and Omni Group's OmniWeb 4.2 support color management, and these only on a Macintosh.

Viewing proofs in Acrobat is more accurate than a browser-based system. Acrobat also lets you attach comments and corrections directly to the PDF file, which you can then return to the printer. This is particularly helpful for collaborative approvals where the same file is passed to different reviewers who make comments in the file. You can also simply print a copy of the PDF file and mark up the hard copy, then return it to the producer.

Soft proofing has two primary advantages — the proof cost is low, and turnaround is rapid. There are, however, several special considerations as well. You have to make sure that your monitor has been properly calibrated and profiled, and that you use the correct output profile to accurately simulate the color of the finished job. Some printers may provide this to you, but most of the time you'll have to use one of the generic CMYK output profiles installed with most graphic-design applications.

Another potential problem associated with soft proofing is related to liability. If your monitor goes out of whack and you approve a job based on its inaccurate display of color, chances are good that the printed product won't be what you expected. Finally, despite the best color-management efforts, it remains difficult to evaluate subtractive-color print media on an emissive additive-color display, simply due to the physics of the two color models. You can get close, but it'll never be an exact match.

Conclusion

Proofing is an essential element of high-quality reproduction. Because a proof is the blueprint to your project, you should check it carefuly before approving either the content or the color. Many designers make the mistake — usually because of the need for quick turnaround — of only glancing at the proof, which is why so many errors appear in final jobs. Careful attention to detail is as important during this final step as it is in the early stages of development.

Glossary

4/1

A job printed with four colors of ink on one side of the sheet, and one color of ink on the other.

4/4

A job printed with four colors of ink on both sides of the sheet. See *Process Colors*, *Subtractive Color*.

Accessibility

The ability for a disabled user to use a Web site.

Achromatic

By definition, having no color; completely black, white, or some shade of gray.

Adaptive Palette

A sampling of colors taken from an image and used in a special compression process, usually to prepare images for the World Wide Web.

Additive Color Process

The process of mixing red, green, and blue light to achieve a wide range of colors, as on a color television screen. See *Subtractive Color*.

Adjacent Color

An adjoining color. Since the eye responds to strong adjoining color, its perception of a particular color is affected by any nearby colors. This means that a color with adjacent colors may look different than it does in isolation.

Algorithm

A specific sequence of mathematical steps to process data. A portion of a computer program that calculates a specific result.

Alpha Channel

An additional channel in an image that defines what parts of the image are transparent or semitransparent. Programs such as Adobe Illustrator, PhotoShop, Premiere, and After Effects use alpha channels to specify transparent regions in an image.

Amplitude-Modulated (AM) Screening

The screening method used to created halftone dot patterns, in which the size of halftone dots vary but the screen ruling and angle remain fixed.

Analog

A signal that fluctuates in exactly the same manner as the original, both in audio and video.

Art

Illustrations and photographs in general. All matter other than text that appears in a mechanical.

Artifact

Something that is artificial or not meant to be there. An artifact can be a blemish or dust spot on a piece of film, or unsightly pixels in a digital image.

ASCII

American Standard Code for Information Interchange. Worldwide, standard ASCII text does not include formatting, and therefore can be exchanged and read by most computer systems.

Autochrome

An early form of color photography, invented by Louis and Auguste Lumiére.

Background

A static object or color that lies behind all other objects.

Banding

A visible stair-stepping of shades in a gradient.

Bandwidth

The transmission capacity, usually measured in bits per second (see BPS), of a network connection.

Bézier Curves

Vector curves that are defined mathematically. These curves can be scaled without the "jaggies" inherent in enlarging bitmapped fonts or graphics.

Binary

Any downloadable file that doesn't simply contain ASCII text. Typically it refers to an executable program available for downloading, but it can also refer to pictures, sounds, or movies, among others.

Binding

In general, the various methods used to secure signatures or leaves in a book. Examples include saddle-stitching (the use of staples in a folded spine), and perfect-bound (multiple sets of folded pages sewn or glued into a flat spine).

Bit (Binary Digit)

A computer's smallest unit of information. Bits can have only two values: 0 or 1.

Bit Depth

A measure of how many colors can be contained in an image. 8-bit color is 256 colors (2 × 2 × 2 × 2 × 2 × 2 × 2 × 2), 16-bit color is 32,768 colors (2 × 2 × 2 × 2 × 2 × 2 × 2 × 2 × 2 × 2 × 2 × 2 × 2 × 2 × 2), and so on.

Bitmap Image

An image constructed from individual dots or pixels set to a grid-like mosaic. The file must contain information about the color and position of each pixel, so the disk space needed for bitmap images can be very large.

Bitmapped

Forming an image with a grid of pixels whose curved edges have discrete steps because of the approximation of the curve due to a finite number pixels.

Black

The absence of color. An ink that absorbs all wavelengths of light.

Blanket

In offset printing, the intermediate step between the printing plate and the substrate. The image is transferred from the plate to a blanket, then from the blanket to the substrate.

Bleed

Page data that extends beyond the trim marks on a page.

Blend

See *Gradient*.

Blow Up

An enlargement, usually of a graphic element such as a photograph.

BMP

A Windows bitmap image format that features low-quality and large file sizes.

Brightness

1. A measure of the amount of light reflected from a surface. 2. A paper property, defined as the percentage reflection of 457-nanometer (nm) radiation. 3. The intensity of a light source. 4. The overall percentage of lightness in an image.

Burn

1. To expose an image onto a plate. 2. To make copies of ROM chips or CD-ROMs. 3. To darken a specific portion of an image through photographic exposure.

Byte

A unit of measure equal to 8 bits (decimal 256) of digital information, sufficient to represent 1 text character. The standard unit measure of file size.

Calibration

Making adjustments to a color monitor and other hardware and software to make the monitor represent as closely as possible the colors of the final production.

Calibration Bars

A strip of color blocks or tonal values on film, proofs, and press sheets, used to check the accuracy of color registration, quality, density, and ink coverage during a print run.

Calotype

An early form of photography, invented by William Henry Fox Talbot, in which paper treated with silver iodide was exposed in a camera.

Camera-Ready

A completely finished mechanical ready to be photographed to produce a negative, from which a printing plate will be made.

CCD

Charge-Coupled Device. A light-sensitive, solid-state semiconductor consisting of image elements (photosites) arranged in a linear or area array. Light illuminates the source, which reflects the light through optics onto the silicon sensors in the array.

Center Marks

Press marks that appear on the center of all sides of a press sheet to aid in positioning the print area on the paper.

Choke

The process in which a lighter background object is extended slightly into a darker foreground object to prevent paper-colored gaps caused by misregistration. See *Trapping*.

Chroma

The degree of saturation of a surface color in the Munsell color space model.

Chromatic Adaptation

The ability of the human visual system to adjust to changes in light and still differentiate colors according to relative saturation.

Chromaticity Diagram

A graphical representation of two of the three dimensions of color. Intended for plotting light sources rather than surface colors. Often called the CIE diagram.

CIE

Commission Internationale de l'Eclairage. An international group that developed a universal set of color definition standards in 1931.

CIE Diagram

See *Chromaticity Diagram*.

Clip Art

Collections of predrawn and digitized graphics.

CMM

Color-Management Module. The engine of a color-management system.

CMS

Color Management System. A process or utility that attempts to manage color of input and output devices in such a way that the monitor will match the output of any CMS-managed printer.

CMYK

Cyan, Magenta, Yellow, Black. The subtractive primaries, or process colors, used in four-color printing.

Color Balance

The combination of yellow, magenta, and cyan needed to produce a neutral gray.

Color Bars

A color standard used by the television industry for the alignment of camera and videotape recordings.

Color Cast

The modification of a hue by the addition of a trace of another hue, such as yellowish green, or pinkish blue. Normally, an unwanted effect that can be corrected.

Color Chart

A printed chart of various combinations of CMYK colors used as an aid for the selection of colors during the design phase of a project.

Color Control Strip

A printed strip of various reference colors used to control printing quality. This strip is normally placed on a press sheet outside the area of a project, used as a guide and visual aid for the press operator.

Color Conversion

Changing the color mode of an image. Converting an image from RGB to CMYK for purposes of preparing the image for conventional printing.

Color Correction

The process of removing casts or unwanted tints in a digital image in an effort to improve the appearance of the image or to correct obvious deficiencies.

Color Depth

Maximum number of colors available for an image. See *Bit Depth*.

Color Gamut

The range of colors that can be formed by all possible combinations of the colorants of a given reproduction system, such as colors that can be displayed on television screens.

Color Key

An overlay color proof of acetate sheets, one for each of the four primary printing inks. The method was developed by 3M Corp. and remains a copyrighted term.

Color Model

A system for describing color, such as RGB, HLS, CIELAB, or CMYK.

Color Overlay

A sheet of film or paper whose text and art correspond to one spot color or process color. Each color overlay becomes the basis for a single printing plate that will apply that color to paper.

Color Picker

A function within a graphics application that assists in selecting or setting a color.

Color Proof

A printed or simulated printed image of the color separations intended to produce a close representation of the final reproduction for approval and as a guide to the press operator.

Color Separation

The process of transforming color artwork into components corresponding to the colors of ink being used, whether process or spot, or a combination of the two.

Color Sequence

The color order of printing the cyan, magenta, yellow, and black inks on a printing press. Sometimes called rotation or color rotation.

Color Shift

The result of compressing out-of-gamut colors into colors that can be reproduced with a given model. Color shift can drastically change the appearance of the final output.

Color Space

A three-dimensional coordinate system in which any color can be represented as a point.

Color Temperature

The temperature, in degrees Kelvin, to which a blackbody would have to be heated to produce a certain color radiation. The graphic arts viewing standard is 5,000 K. The norm for television lighting is 3,200 K, and for outdoors is 5,600 K.

Colorimeter

An optical measuring instrument designed to measure and quantify color. It is often used to match digital image values to those of cloth and other physical samples.

Commercial Printing

Typically, printing on high-capacity, high-resolution presses; processes include offset lithography, flexography, gravure, and screen printing. Offset printing is the most widely used commercial printing process.

Comp

Comprehensive artwork used to present the general color and layout of a page.

Complementary Color

Opposite colors on the color wheel.

Composite Proof

A version of an illustration or page in which the process colors appear together to represent full color. When produced on a monochrome output device, colors are represented as shades of gray.

Compression

A technique used to reduce file size by analyzing occurrences of similar data. Compressed files occupy less space, and their use improves digital transmission speeds. Compression can sometimes result in a loss of image quality and/or resolution.

Continuous Tone

An image (such as a photograph) in which the subject has continuous shades of color or gray tones through the use of an emulsion process. Continuous tone images must be screened to create halftone images to be printed.

Contrast

The relationship and degree of difference between the dark and light areas of an image.

Crop Marks

Printed lines used as guides for final trimming of the pages within a press sheet.

Daguerreotype

An early form of photography, invented by Louis Daguerre, in which a silver plate was exposed to iodine vapor to create a light-sensitive surface on the plate.

DCS

Desktop Color Separation. A version of the EPS file format. DCS 1.0 is composed of five files for each color image plus a separate low-resolution image to place in a digital file. DCS 2.0 has one file that stores process and spot color information.

Demographics

Audience research factors concerned with such items as age, gender, marital status, and income.

Densitometer

An electronic instrument used to measure optical density; reflective for paper, and transmissive for film.

Density

The ability of a material to absorb light. In film, it refers to the opacity of an area of the image. A maximum density of 4.0 refers to solid black. Improper density in film results in washed-out or overly-dark reproduction.

Descreening

A technique used to obscure the halftone dot pattern when scanning printed material.

Device-Dependent Color

Reproduction in which output color is determined by the output device characteristics.

Device-Independent Color

Reproduction in which output color is absolute, and is not determined by the output device characteristics.

DICColor

A special-color library commonly used in Japan.

Die Line

The outline used to mark where cutting, stamping, or embossing the finished printed piece will occur. Used to create a particular shape, such as a rolodex card.

Digital

The use of a series of discrete electronic pulses to represent data. In digital imaging systems, 256 steps (8 bits, or 1 byte) are normally used to characterize the gray scale or the properties of 1 color.

Digital Camera

A camera that produces images directly into an electronic file format for transfer to a computer.

Direct-to-Plate

Producing printing plates or other image carriers from computer output, usually via laser exposure, without an intermediate film exposure.

Dithering

A technique in which a color is represented using dots of two different colors displayed or printed very close together. Dithering is often used to compress digital images and in special screening algorithms.

Dmax

The maximum density in an image, or the maximum density that can be captured with a scanner or digital camera.

Dmin

The minimum density in an image, or the minimum density that can be captured with a scanner or digital camera.

Dot Gain

The growth of a halftone dot that occurs whenever ink soaks into paper. Failure to compensate for this gain in the generation of digital images can result in very poor results on press. Also known as "tone value increase."

Dot Pitch

In computer monitors, the distance (in millimeters) between the holes in the shadow mask: the smaller the number, the sharper the image. Generally, the smaller the number, the higher the resolution of a given monitor size.

DPI

Dots Per Inch. The measurement of resolution for page printers, phototypesetting machines, and graphics screens. Currently graphics screens use resolutions of 72 to 96 dpi; standard desktop laser printers work at 600 dpi.

Drum Scanner

A color scanner on which the original is wrapped around a rotary scanning drum. See *Scanner*.

Duotone

The separation of a photograph into black and a second color. Duotones are used to enhance photographic reproduction in two-, three-, or sometimes four-color work. Often the second, third, and fourth colors are not standard CMYK inks.

Dye Transfer

A photographic color print using special coated papers to produce a full color image. Can serve as an inexpensive proof.

Dynamic Range

The difference between the lightest and darkest area of an image. Also used to describe the range of color capture capability in a scanner or digital camera.

Effective Resolution

The final resolution of an image, calculated by dividing the image resolution (pixels per inch) by the magnification percentage.

Elliptical Dot Screen

A halftone screen having an elliptical dot structure.

Emulsion

The coating of light-sensitive material (silver halide) on a piece of film or photographic paper.

EPS

Encapsulated PostScript. File format used to transfer PostScript data within compatible applications. EPS files can contain text, vector artwork, and images.

File Compression

The process of reducing the number of bytes in a file, file compression is usually used when transferring files between computers.

Film

Non-paper output of an imagesetter or phototypesetter.

Flat Color

Color that lacks contrast or tonal variation. Also called flat tint.

Flatbed Scanner

A scanner on which the original is mounted on a flat scanning glass. See *Scanner*.

Flexographic Printing

A rotary letterpress printing process using a rubber plate that stretches around a cylinder making it necessary to compensate by distorting the plate image. Flexography is used most often for printing on metal or other non-paper material.

Focoltone

A special-color library used in the United States.

Folding Dummy

A template used for determining the page arrangement on a form to meet folding and binding requirements.

Four-Color Process

Process color printer. See *Process Colors*.

FPO

For Position Only. A term applied to low-quality images or simple shapes used to indicate placement and scaling of an art element on mechanicals or camera-ready artwork.

Frequency-Modulated (FM) Screening

A method of creating halftones in which the size of the dots remains constant but their density is varied; also known as stochastic screening.

Gamma

A measure of the contrast, or range of tonal variation of the midtones in a photographic image.

Gamma Correction

1. Adjusting the contrast of the midtones in an image. 2. Calibrating a monitor so midtones are correctly displayed on screen.

Gamut

See *Color Gamut*.

Gamut Shift

See *Color Shift*.

GCR

See *Gray Component Replacement*.

Generation

The number of steps away from the original. The original is first-generation; a scan of the original is second-generation; a scan of a print of the original is third-generation.

GIF

Graphics Interchange Format. A popular graphics format for online clip art and drawn graphics. Graphics in this format are acceptable at low resolution. See *JPEG*.

GRACoL

General Requirements for Applications in Commercial Offset Lithography. Created by the Graphic Communications Association, a document containing general guidelines and recommendations for achieving quality color printing.

Gradient

A gradual transition from one color to another. The shape of the gradient and the proportion of the two colors can be varied. Also known as blends, gradations, graduated fills, and vignettes.

Grain

Silver salts clumped together in differing amounts in different types of photographic emulsions. Generally speaking, faster emulsions have larger grain sizes.

Graininess

Visual impression of the irregularly distributed silver grain clumps in a photographic image, or the ink film in a printed image.

Graphics

All visuals specially prepared for the television screen, such as title cards, charts, and graphs.

Gray Balance

The values for the yellow, magenta, and cyan inks that are needed to produce a neutral gray when printed at a normal density.

Gray Component Replacement

A technique for adding detail by reducing the amount of cyan, magenta and yellow in chromatic or colored areas, replacing them with black.

Grayscale

1. An image composed in grays ranging from black to white, usually using 256 different tones. 2. A tint ramp used to measure and control the accuracy of screen percentages. 3. An accessory used to define neutral density in a photographic image.

Halftone

An image generated for use in printing in which a range of continuous tones is simulated by an array of dots that create the illusion of continuous tone when seen at a distance.

Halftone Tint

An area covered with a uniform halftone dot size to produce an even tone or color. Also called flat tint or screen tint.

Heraldry

The formal development of official family identity devices.

Hex Values

Numbers specified in the hexadecimal system, commonly used for specifying colors on Web pages.

Hexachrome

Six-color printing process developed by PANTONE, in which green and orange are added to the process colors to extend the printable gamut. Also called "HiFi."

High Key

A photographic or printed image in which the main interest area lies in the highlight end of the scale.

Highlight

The lightest areas in a photograph or illustration.

High-Resolution File

An image file that typically contains four pixels for every dot in the printed reproduction. High-resolution files are often linked to a page-layout file, but not actually embedded in it, due to their large size.

HLS

A color model based on three coordinates: hue, lightness (luminance), and saturation.

HSL

A color model that defines color based on its hue, saturation, and luminosity (value), as it is displayed on a video or computer screen.

HSV

A color model based on three coordinates: hue, saturation, and value (or luminance).

Hue

The wavelength of light of a color in its purest state (without adding white or black).

ICC

International Color Consortium. A standards-making body for color reproduction technology.

Illumination

Hand-drawn illustration, often in color, that was added to medieval manuscripts.

Imagesetter

A raster-based device used to output a digital file at high resolution (usually 1000–3000 dpi) onto photographic paper or film, from which printing plates are made, or directly to printing plates (called a "platesetter").

Impression Cylinder

In commercial printing, a cylinder that provides back pressure, thus allowing the image to be transferred from the blanket to the substrate.

Indexed Color Image

An image that uses a limited, predetermined number of colors; often used in Web images. See also *GIF*.

Ink Film Thickness

The amount of ink that is transferred to the substrate.

Intensity

Synonym for degree of color saturation.

Interpolated Resolution

"Artificial" resolution that is created by averaging the color and intensity of adjacent pixels. Commonly used in scanning to achieve resolution higher than the scanner' optical resolution.

Jaggies

Visible steps in the curved edge of a graphic or text character that result from enlarging a bitmapped image.

JPEG

A compression algorithm that reduces the file size of bitmapped images, named for the Joint Photographic Experts Group, which created the standard. JPEG is "lossy" compression; image quality is reduced in direct proportion to the amount of compression.

Kelvin (K)

Unit of temperature measurement based on Celsius degrees, starting from absolute zero, equivalent to -273 Celsius (centigrade); used to indicate the color temperature of a light source.

Key

1. Principal source of illumination. High- or low-key lighting. 2. Also an electronic effect (example: chroma key).

Knockout

A printing technique that prints overlapping objects without mixing inks. The ink for the underlying element does not print (knocks out) in the area where the objects overlap. Opposite of overprinting.

L*a*b*

The lightness, red-green attribute, and yellow-blue attribute in the CIE L*a*b* color space, a three-dimensional color mapping system.

Lightness

The property that distinguishes white from gray or black, and light from dark color tones on a surface.

Line Art

A drawing or piece of black-and-white artwork with no screens. Line art can be represented by a graphic file having only 1-bit resolution.

Line Screen

See *LPI*.

Lithography

A mechanical printing process based on the principle of the natural aversion of water to grease. In modern offset lithography, the image on a photosensitive plate is first transferred to the blanket of a rotating drum, and then to the paper.

Lossy

A data compression method characterized by the loss of some data.

LPI

Lines Per Inch. The number of lines per inch used when converting a photograph to a halftone. Typical values range from 85 for newspaper work to 150 or higher for high-quality reproduction on smooth or coated paper. Also called "line screen."

Luminosity

The amount of light or brightness in an image. Part of the HLS color model.

LUT

Look-Up Table. A chart of numbers that describe the color reproduction characteristics of a specific device.

Lux

European standard unit for measuring light intensity: 1 lux is the amount of 1 lumen (one candlepower of light).

LZW Compression

Lempel-ziy-welch compression. A method of reducing the size of image files.

Makeready

The process of starting a printing press and manipulating the controls until the press is running at its optimum capability.

Masking

A technique used to display certain areas of an image or design; the shape and size of the top-most object or layer defines what is visible on lower layers.

Match Print

A color proofing system used for the final quality check.

Mechanical

A pasted-up page of camera-ready art that is photographed to produce a plate for the press.

Mechanical Dot Gain

See *Dot Gain*.

Medium

A physical carrier of data such as a CD-ROM, video cassette, or floppy disk, or a carrier of electronic data such as fiber optic cable or electric wires.

Memory Color

The tendency to evaluate color based on what we expect to see rather than what is actually there.

Metallic Ink

Printing inks which produce gold, silver, bronze, or metallic colors.

Metamerism

Phenomenon in which the same color appears differently in different lighting conditions.

Midtones

The tonal range between highlights and shadows. Also called "middletones."

Minimum Printable Dot

The smallest dot that can be accurately and consistently reproduced on film or a printing plate.

Misregister

The unwanted result of incorrectly aligned process inks and spot colors on a finished printed piece. Misregistration can be caused by many factors, including paper stretch and improper plate alignment. Trapping can compensate for misregistration.

Moiré

An interference pattern caused by the overlap of two or more regular patterns such as dots or lines. In process-color printing, screen angles are selected to minimize this pattern.

Monochrome

An image or computer monitor in which all information is represented in black and white, or with a range of grays.

Mottle

Uneven color or tone.

Named Colors

A set of colors specifically designated for reference by name, rather than by RGB or hexadecimal values.

Neutral

Any color that is absent of hue, such as white, gray, or black.

Neutral Density

A measurement of the lightness or darkness of a color. A neutral density of zero (0.00) is the lightest value possible, and is equivalent to pure white; 3.294 is roughly equivalent to 100% of each of the CMYK components.

Noise

Unwanted signals or data that can reduce the quality of output. On a television screen, it resembles snow.

Non-Reproducible Colors

Colors in an original scene or photograph that are impossible to reproduce using process inks. Also called out-of-gamut colors.

Normal Key

A description of an image in which the main interest area is in the middle range of the tone scale, or distributed throughout the entire tonal range.

Offset Lithography

A printing method whereby the image is transferred from a plate onto a rubber-covered cylinder, from which the printing takes place. See *Lithography*.

Opacity

1. The degree to which paper will show print through it. 2. The degree to which images or text below one object, whose opacity has been adjusted, are able to show through.

Optical Resolution

The actual resolution of a scanner's optics. See also *Interpolated Resolution*.

Out-of-Gamut

Color that cannot be reproduced with a specific color model. Many RGB colors fall outside the CMYK gamut.

Output Device

Any hardware equipment, such as a monitor, laser printer, or imagesetter, that depicts text or graphics created on a computer.

Overlay

A transparent sheet used in the preparation of multicolor mechanical artwork showing the color breakdown.

Overprint Color

A color made by overprinting any two or more of the primary yellow, magenta, and cyan process colors.

Overprinting

Allowing an element to print over the top of underlying elements, rather than knocking them out (see *Knockout*). Often used with black type.

Palette

1. As derived from the term in the traditional art world, a collection of selectable colors. 2. Another name for a dialog box or menu of choices.

PANTONE Matching System

PMS. A system for specifying colors by number for both coated and uncoated paper; used by print services and in color desktop publishing to assure uniform color matching.

PDF

Portable Document Format. Developed by Adobe Systems, Inc. (read by Acrobat Reader), this format has become a de facto standard for document transfer across platforms.

Perfecting Press

A commercial printing press configuration, in which both sides of the substrate are printed at one time.

Photomechanical Transfer (PMT)

Positive prints of text or images used for paste-up to mechanicals.

Photomultiplier Tube

Very sensitive color-capture technology used in high-end drum scanners.

PICT/PICT2

A common format for defining bitmapped images on the Macintosh. The more recent PICT2 format supports 24-bit color.

Pixel

Picture Element. One of the tiny rectangular areas or dots generated by a computer or output device to constitute images. A greater number of pixels per inch results in higher resolution on screen or in print.

PNG

Portable Network Graphics. PNG is a new graphics format similar to GIF. It is a relatively new file format, and is not yet widely supported by most browsers.

Positive

A true photographic image of the original made on paper or film.

Posterize, Posterization

1. Deliberate constraint of a gradient or image into visible steps as a special effect. 2. Unintentional creation of steps in an image due to a high lpi (lines per inch) value used with a low dpi (dots per inch) printer.

PPI

Pixels Per Inch. Used to denote the resolution of an image.

Primary Colors

Colors that can be used to generate secondary colors. For the additive system (a computer monitor), these colors are red, green, and blue. For the subtractive system (the printing process), these colors are yellow, magenta, and cyan.

Process Colors

The four inks (cyan, magenta, yellow, and black) used in four-color process printing. A printing method in which a full range of colors is reproduced by combining four semi-transparent inks. See *Color Separation, CMYK.*

Profile

A file containing data representing the color reproduction characteristics of a device determined by a calibration of some sort.

Proof

A representation of the printed job that is made from plates (press proof), film, or electronic data (prepress proofs). It is generally used for customer inspection and approval before mass production begins.

Raster

A bitmapped representation of graphic data.

Raster Graphics

A class of graphics created and organized in a rectangular array of bitmaps. Often created by paint software or scanners.

Rasterize

The process of converting digital information into pixels. For example, the process used by an imagesetter to translate PostScript files before they are imaged to film or paper.

Reflective Art

Artwork that is opaque, as opposed to transparent, that can be scanned for input to a computer.

Registration

Aligning plates on a multicolor printing press so the images will superimpose properly to produce the required composite output.

Registration Color

A default color selection that can be applied to design elements so they will print on every separation from a PostScript printer. "Registration" is often used to print identification text that will appear outside the page area on a set of separations.

Registration Marks

Figures (often crossed lines and a circle) placed outside the trim page boundaries on all color separation overlays to provide a common element for proper alignment.

Rendering Intent

The method used to convert color from one space to another.

Repurposing

Converting an existing document for another different use; usually refers to creating an electronic version of existing print publications.

Resample

Resizing an image to decrease the physical size of the file, not just change the appearance on the page.

Resolution

The density of graphic information expressed in dots per inch (dpi) or pixels per inch (ppi).

RGB

1. The colors of projected light from a computer monitor that, when combined, simulate a subset of the visual spectrum.
2. The color model of most digital artwork. See also *CMYK.*

Rich Black

A process color consisting of solid black with one or more layers of cyan, magenta, or yellow. Also called "superblack."

RIP

Raster Image Processor. That part of a PostScript printer or imagesetting device that converts the page information from the PostScript Page Description Language into the bitmap pattern that is applied to the film or paper output.

Rosette

The pattern created when color halftone screens are printed at traditional screen angles.

Rubylith

A two-layer acetate film having a red or amber emulsion on a clear base used in non-computer stripping and separation operations.

Saturation

The intensity or purity of a color; a color with no saturation is gray.

Scaling

The means within a program to reduce or enlarge the amount of space an image occupies by multiplying the data by a factor. Scaling can be proportional, or in one dimension only.

Scanner

A device that electronically digitizes images on a point-by-point basis through circuits that can correct color, manipulate tones, and enhance detail.

Screen

To create a halftone of a continuous-tone image.

Screen Angle

The angle at which the rulings of a halftone screen are set when making halftones for commercial printing.

Screen Frequency

The number of lines per inch in a halftone screen, which may vary from 85 to 300.

Screen Ruling

See *LPI.*

Secondary Color

The result of mixing two primary colors. In additive (RGB) color, cyan, magenta, and yellow are the secondary colors. In subtractive (CMY) color, red, green, and blue are the secondary colors.

Selective Color

The addition of color to certain elements of a grayscale image, usually to draw attention to the colored object or area.

Separation

The process of preparing individual color components for commercial printing. Each ink color is reproduced as a unique piece of film or printing plate.

Service Bureau

An organization that provides services, such as scanning and prepress checks, that prepare your publication to be printed on a commercial printing press. Service bureaus do not, however, print your publication.

Shade

A color mixed with black: a 10% shade is one part of the original color and nine parts black. See Tint.

Sharpness

The subjective impression of the density difference between two tones at their boundary, interpreted as fineness of detail.

Special Color

Colors that are reproduced using premixed inks, often used to print colors that are outside the CMYK gamut.

Spectral Absorption

Light wavelengths that are absorbed by the pigments in an object's surface.

Spectral Output

Color balance.

Spectral Reflectance

Light wavelengths that are not absorbed by the pigments in an object's surface.

Spectrophotometer

A device used to precisely measure the wavelengths that are reflected from an object's surface.

Specular Highlight

The lightest highlight area that does not carry any detail, such as reflections from glass or polished metal. Normally, these areas are reproduced as unprinted white paper.

SPI

Samples per inch. Term used to describe the imaging capabilities of a scanner.

SPI

Spots per inch. The number of dots created by an imagesetter or platesetter in one linear inch. Often used interchangeably with "dots per inch."

Spot Color

Any pre-mixed ink that is not one of the four process-color inks.

Spot-Color Printing

The printing method in which special ink colors are used independently or in conjunction with process colors to create a specific color that is outside the gamut of process-color printing.

Spread

1. Two abutting pages. 2. A trapping process that slightly enlarges a lighter foreground object to prevent white paper gaps caused by misregistration.

Stochastic Screening

See *Frequency-Modulated (FM) Screening*.

Stripping

The act of manually assembling individual film negatives into flats for printing. Also referred to as "film assembly.

Substrate

Any surface that is being printed.

Subtractive Color

Color that is observed when light strikes pigments or dyes, which absorb certain wavelengths of light; the light that is reflected back is perceived as a color. See *CMYK, Process Color*.

Superblack

See *Rich Black*.

SWOP

Specifications for Web Offset Publications. Industry standards for web-offset printing; SWOP specifications provide the necessary information to produce consistent high-quality printing.

TAC

Total Area Coverage. The maximum amount of ink that can be printed in a single area. Also called "total ink density."

TIFF

Tagged Image File Format. A common format used for scanned or computer-generated bitmapped images.

Tone Value Increase

See *Dot Gain*.

Total Ink Density

See *TAC*.

Toyo

A special-color library commonly used in Japan.

Transfer Curve

A curve depicting the adjustment to be made to a particular printing plate when an image is printed.

Transparency

1. A full-color photographically-produced image on transparent film. 2. The quality of an image element that allows background elements to partially or entirely show through.

Transparent Ink

An ink that allows light to be transmitted through it.

Trapping

The process of creating an overlap between abutting inks to compensate for imprecise registration in the printing process. Extending the lighter colors of one object into the darker colors of an adjoining object.

Trumatch

A special-color library used in the U.S.

Undercolor Removal (UCR)

A technique for reducing the amount of magenta, cyan, and yellow inks in neutral or shadow areas and replacing them with black.

Undertone

Color of ink printed in a thin film.

Unsharp Masking

A digital technique performed after scanning that locates the edge between sections of differing lightness and alters the values of the adjoining pixels to exaggerate the difference across the edge, thereby increasing edge contrast.

Varnish Plate

The plate on a printing press that applies varnish after the other colors have been applied.

Vector Graphics

Graphics defined using coordinate points and mathematically drawn lines and curves, which may be freely scaled and rotated without image degradation in the final output.

Video Card

The graphics card that ships with your computer. The graphics card is responsible for enabling the display or monitor in your computer setup. You can upgrade to a more powerful video card based on the configuration of your computer.

Vignette

An illustration in which the background gradually fades into the paper; that is, without a definite edge or border.

Visible Spectrum

The wavelengths of light between about 380 nm (violet) and 700 nm (red) that are visible to the human eye.

Web-Safe Color

A color palette used for images that will be displayed on the Internet. The Web-safe color palette is a specific set that can be displayed by most computer-operating systems and monitors.

White Balance

Equal amounts of red, green, and blue light components to create white.

White Light

Light containing all wavelengths of the visible spectrum. Also known as 5000K lighting.

XYZ

A device-independent color system developed by the CIE; the predecessor to CIE L*a*b*.

Index

T

U

V

W